THE GOSPEL:
GOD, MAN, & TRUTH

By David H. Yarn, Jr.

CLASSICS IN MORMON
LITERATURE
Deseret Book Company
Salt Lake City, Utah
1979

Library of Congress Catalog Card No. 65-18575
ISBN 0-87747-718-3

To Karen, Steffani, Rebecca,
Teresa, Jennifer, and Joanna

PREFACE

These chapters have been written over a period of perhaps twelve years. The only ones which were written expressly to be published sequentially are chapters 1 through 5. The others have been written for various occasions as articles for periodicals, or formal papers for special seminars or assemblies, etc. Although they have been written over a period of years and according to no predetermined plan, they do constitute a remarkably coherent sequence as arranged for this book.

The title of this work, *The Gospel: God, Man, and Truth*, is a generic description of its contents. Chapters 1 through 5 deal principally with the Godhead: Elohim, the Father; Jesus Christ, the Redeemer; and the Holy Ghost, the Comforter. Chapters 6 through 13 deal principally with man. And chapters 14 through 17 deal primarily with truth.

Although the specific content of each chapter is indicated in its own title, there is also an implicit relationship of all three of the major and underlying concerns of this book in each chapter too. In the concluding chapter, "Ye Shall Know the Truth . . ." there is a convergence of these concerns, God, Man, and Truth.

It is the hope of the author that this book will be of interest and value to any reader, but particularly that it will be of assistance to the student whose mind is frequently challenged with new and enticing—sometimes beguiling—ideas, in helping him to be firmly anchored in the gospel of Jesus Christ.

Through the years I have discussed various parts of the contents of this book with different ones of my colleagues and I would like to express appreciation to them for their influence, encouragement, and assistance. I am indebted to Drs. Sidney B. Sperry, B. West

Belnap, Chauncey C. Riddle, Truman G. Madsen, and Professor Robert K. Thomas. I am especially indebted to Professor Roy W. Doxey, who has examined the entire manuscript. Thanks is also due my wife, Marilyn, three of my daughters, Karen, Steffani and Rebecca, and my secretary, Miss Pauline Duke. Mr. Alva H. Parry of Deseret Book Company and his staff have made helpful suggestions and have been most cooperative, and I also wish to acknowledge here my appreciation for their assistance.

PUBLISHER'S PREFACE TO THE 1978 CLASSICS IN MORMON LITERATURE SERIES EDITION

The Gospel: God, Man, and Truth is a book that is unique in our Mormon literature. In its discussions of those three topics—God, man, and truth—it helps clarify and create perspective for all readers, and especially for the student of philosophy and religion who stretches his mind to understand the philosophy of the world as it relates to the restored gospel of Jesus Christ.

Because this work has been published in the Classics in Mormon Literature series, we have not attempted to correct numbers and data that were current in the 1965 edition. Also, where the author has quoted materials that are now part of the new scriptures added to the Pearl of Great Price in 1976 we have left the original reference.

CONTENTS

ABBREVIATIONS

The Standard Works of The Church of Jesus Christ
of Latter-day Saints:

The Holy Bible: Books of the Bible.

The Book of Mormon: 1 Nephi
2 Nephi   (These
Mosiah   are the only
Alma   books cited
Mormon   in the Book
Ether   of Mor-
Moroni   mon.)

The Doctrine and Covenants: D&C   The sections are referred
to by their respective numbers

The Pearl of Great Price: Moses
Abraham
Joseph Smith

Abbreviations for other works cited in this book:

AF   *The Articles of Faith* (Sixteenth edition in English),
by James E. Talmage.

CR   Reports of Annual and Semiannual Conferences of The
Church of Jesus Christ of Latter-day Saints.

DBY   *Discourses of Brigham Young* (1941 edition), edited by
John A. Widtsoe.

DHC   *Documentary History of the Church,* or *History of the
Church of Jesus Christ of Latter-day Saints,* by
Joseph Smith, edited by B. H. Roberts.

DS   *Doctrines of Salvation,* by Joseph Fielding Smith, compiled by Bruce R. McConkie.

GD   *Gospel Doctrine* (Fifth edition), by Joseph F. Smith.

JD   *Journal of Discourses* (26 volumes).

TPJS   *Teachings of the Prophet Joseph Smith,* compiled by
Joseph Fielding Smith.

Other sources, which are referred to less frequently in this work,
are identified in appropriate places in the text.

PART I   GOD

CHAPTER I

ELOHIM

Through the ages peoples of all times, places, and cultures have speculated much regarding and been very concerned about the notion of God.

The very influential German philosopher, Georg Wilhelm Friedrich Hegel (d. 1831) makes an extremely important observation concerning this interest of mankind in the following passage:

> Religion is the sphere in which a nation gives itself the definition of that which it regards as the True. A definition contains everything that belongs to the essence of an object; reducing its nature to its simple characteristic predicate, as a mirror for every predicate — the generic soul pervading all its details. The conception of God, therefore, constitutes the general basis of a people's character. (*The Philosophy of History* [Revised Edition; New York: Willey Book Co., 1944], p. 50.)

As one considers Hegel's statement it could be a very profitable enterprise for him to ask himself what he *thinks* about God, *believes* about God, and *knows* about God, and how his answers to these questions influence his life.

God has revealed much regarding himself through his prophets, particularly in our dispensation. Let us examine some of the things he has revealed about himself and what they should mean to us in terms of our own conduct or behavior.

The Meaning of "Elohim"

"Elohim" is a name for God which is found in Hebrew texts of the Old Testament. It is the plural form of "El" and "Eloah," other Semitic words for God. Not only does "Elohim" have a quantitative meaning but a qualitative meaning as well. That is, not only does it mean "Gods" instead of "God" but it also connotes maj-

esty, excellence, power, and supremacy. It is in this
latter sense that "Elohim" is used as the name of God
the Eternal Father. The name is representative of his
greatness.

God Is an Exalted Man

Speaking of Elohim, the Prophet Joseph Smith declared:

*God himself was once as we are now, and is an exalted man,
and sits enthroned in yonder heavens. That is the great secret.
If the veil were rent today, and the great God who holds this
world in its orbit, and who upholds all worlds and all things
by his power, was to make himself visible, — I say, if you
were to see him today, you would see him like a man in form
— like yourselves in all the person, image, and very form as
a man; for Adam was created in the very fashion, image and
likeness of God, and received instructions from, and walked,
talked and conversed with him, as one man talks and communes
with another.*

* * *

*. . . It is the first principle of the Gospel to know for a cer-
tainty the character of God, and to know that we may converse
with him as one man converses with another, and that he was
once a man like us; yea, that God himself, the Father of us
all, dwelt on an earth, the same as Jesus Christ himself did. . . .*
(TPJS:345-346.)

Mortals are not treading a course unknown to God.
He knows mortality not merely analogically or even vi-
cariously but by his own personal experience.

He has not chosen to reveal himself personally to
men upon the earth many times, but he has done so
sufficiently that man should know both that he is, and
what he is.

He bore witness with his voice, of Jesus' divine
Sonship at Jesus' baptism. (Màtthew 3:17.)

On the mount of transfiguration the three chief
apostles, after beholding the transfigured Lord and

Moses and Elijah, heard the Father identify Jesus as his beloved Son. (Matthew 17:5.) Again, after Jesus entered Jerusalem for the last week of his mortal life, the Father's voice was heard (and interpreted variously) by the people, in response to Jesus' prayer unto him. (John 12:28.)

But the Father has *shown* himself to some of his mortal children. As Stephen was being stoned to death he saw the Father in vision. (Acts 7:55-56.) The young Joseph Smith saw him in his first vision. (*Joseph Smith* 2:17.) Also Sidney Rigdon in the company of Joseph Smith saw the Father. (D&C 76:20-24.)

Joseph Smith, in relating his first vision, speaks of God as a personage who spoke to him. In section 130 of the Doctrine and Covenants, which contains "Important Items of Instruction given by Joseph Smith the Prophet," it is declared that "The Father has a body of flesh and bones as tangible as man's." (vs. 22.) Further, when Paul wrote to the Hebrews and bore his testimony of Jesus as the Son he described him as being in the express image of the Father's person. (Hebrews 1:1-3.)

It is also interesting and significant to observe that during the creation God declared, "Let us make man in our image, after our likeness," and that the record says "So God created man in his own image, in the image of God created he him; male and female created he them." (Genesis 1:26-27.) But this is made even more meaningful when we note the record regarding the birth of Adam's son, Seth. It reads: "This is the book of the generations of Adam. In the day that God created man, in the likeness of God made he him. . . . And Adam lived an hundred and thirty years, and begat a son in his own likeness, after his image; and called his name Seth." (*Ibid.*, 5:1-3.) That is, Adam was in the image of God and after his likeness, and Seth was in the image of Adam and after his likeness.

Therefore, Elohim, or God the Eternal Father, is not some vague abstraction. He is not a mystical something or other which can dwell in the hearts of men. As the Prophet Joseph Smith said, "the idea that the Father and the Son dwell in a man's heart is an old sectarian notion, and is false." (D&C 130:3.) On the contrary, he is a personal being. As President Brigham Young said:

> If we could see our heavenly Father, we should see a being similar to our earthly parent, with this difference, our Father in heaven is exalted and glorified. (*JD* 4:54, Sept. 21, 1856.)

God's Knowledge, Character, and Other Attributes

Abraham understood the foregoing very well, for he said, "Thus I, Abraham, talked with the Lord, face to face, as one man talketh with another; and he told me of the works which his hands had made; And he said unto me: My son, my son (and his hand was stretched out), behold I will show you all these. And he put his hand upon mine eyes, and I saw those things which his hands had made, which were many; and they multiplied before mine eyes and I could not see the end thereof." (Abraham 3:1-12.)

While Abraham enjoyed that great experience with God he was told something of tremendous importance regarding God himself. Abraham relates: "And the Lord said unto me: These two facts do exist, that there are two spirits, one being more intelligent than the other; there shall be another more intelligent than they; I am the Lord thy God, I am more intelligent than they all." (*Ibid.*, 3:19.)

In this dispensation it has been revealed that God's glory is intelligence. One should not assume, however, that this connotes mental brilliance only, for the revelation continues by identifying intelligence as light and truth, and declares, "Light and truth forsake that evil one." (D&C 93:36-37.) This suggests that the intelligence which is God's glory is not only intellectual capacity and knowledge but a disposition of character. It is a disposition which is contrary to evil.

The Prophet Joseph Smith in describing the Father's knowledge and character said: "God is the only supreme governor and independent being in whom all fullness and perfection dwell; who is omnipotent, omnipresent and omniscient; without beginning of days or end of life; and that in him every good gift and every good principle dwell; and that he is the Father of lights; in him the principle of faith dwells independently, and he is the object in whom the faith of all other rational and accountable beings center for life and salvation." (*Lectures on Faith* [Salt Lake City: N. B. Lundwall, compiler and publisher, no date] Lecture 2, para. 2.)

> . . . Without the knowledge of all things, God would not be able to save any portion of his creatures; for it is by reason of the knowledge which he has of all things, from the beginning to the end, that enables him to give that understanding to his creatures by which they are made partakers of eternal life; and if it were not for the idea existing in the minds of men that God had all knowledge it would be impossible for them to exercise faith in him. (Lec. 4, para. 11.)

After enumerating and briefly discussing some of God's attributes, the Prophet summarized in these words:

> Let the mind once reflect sincerely and candidly upon the ideas of the existence of the before-mentioned attributes in the Deity, and it will be seen that, as far as his attributes are concerned, there is a sure foundation laid for the exercise of faith in him for life and salvation. For inasmuch as God possesses the attribute knowledge, he can make all things known to his saints necessary for their salvation; and as he possesses the attribute power, he is able thereby to deliver them from the power of all enemies; and seeing, also, that justice is an attribute of the Deity, he will deal with them upon the principles of

righteousness and equity, and a just reward will be granted unto them for all their afflictions and sufferings for the truth's sake. And as judgment is an attribute of the Deity also, his saints can have the most unshaken confidence that they will, in due time, obtain a perfect deliverance out of the hands of their enemies, and a complete victory over all those who have sought their hurt and destruction. And as mercy is also an attribute of the Deity, his saints can have confidence that it will be exercised towards them, and through the exercise of that attribute towards them comfort and consolation will be administered unto them abundantly, amid all their afflictions and tribulations. And, lastly, realizing that truth is an attribute of the Deity, the mind is led to rejoice amid all its trials and temptations, in hope of that glory which is to be brought at the revelation of Jesus Christ, and in view of that crown which is to be placed upon the heads of the saints in the day when the Lord shall distribute rewards unto them, and in prospect of that eternal weight of glory which the Lord has promised to bestow upon them, when he shall bring them in the midst of his throne to dwell in his presence eternally. (Lec. 4, para. 17.)

Inasmuch as these are some of the attributes of your Father, to what extent are you developing these attributes in yourself? Do you *really* want to become as he is?

More briefly than the Prophet Joseph Smith, Alma epitomizes God's attributes as follows: "He has all power, all wisdom, and all understanding; he comprehendeth all things, and he is a merciful Being even unto salvation, to those who will repent and believe on his name." (Alma 26:35.)

Law in the Cosmos

Concerning the vast creations of the cosmos and the application of God's knowledge, power, and benevolence, he has revealed the following: "All kingdoms have a law given; and there are many kingdoms; for there is no space in the which there is no kingdom; and there is no kingdom in the which there is no space, either a greater or a lesser kingdom. And unto every kingdom is given a law; and unto every law there are certain bounds also and conditions." (D&C 88:36-38.)

Speaking of the Father, the revelation continues, "He hath given a law unto all things, by which they move in their times and their seasons; And their courses are fixed, even the courses of the heavens and the earth, which comprehend the earth and all the planets." (*Ibid.*, 88:42-43.)

Elohim Is Our Father

The existence of the earth, the moon, other planets, the sun, and the countless vast systems of the cosmos as the works of Elohim justify his majestic name. However, these great things do not entitle him to the name Eternal or Heavenly Father except metaphorically. But his being called Father does not rest upon this metaphorical entitlement, for he is literally the Father of the spirits of all mankind.

President Brigham Young said:

I want to tell you, each and every one of you, that you are well acquainted with God our heavenly Father, or the great Elohim. You are all well acquainted with Him, for there is not a soul of you but what has lived in His house and dwelt with Him year after year; and yet you are seeking to become acquainted with Him, when the fact is, you have merely forgotten what you did know . . . .

There is not a person here today but what is a son or a daughter of that Being. In the spirit world their spirits were first begotten and brought forth, and they lived there with their parents for ages before they came here. This, perhaps, is hard for many to believe, but it is the greatest nonsense in the world not to believe it. If you do not believe it, cease to call Him Father; and when you pray, pray to some other character. (*JD* 4:216, February 8, 1857.)

Man is the offspring of God. . . . We are as much the children of this great Being as we are the children of our mortal progenitors. (*Ibid.*, 9:283, February 23, 1862.)

President George Albert Smith spoke similarly when he said:

. . . we are the children of God. He is the Father of our spirits. We have not come from some lower form of life, but God is the Father of our spirits, and we belong to the royal family, because He is our Father. (*CR*, p. 125, April, 1946.)

The realization that we are of a celestial parentage should so inspire men and women that they should not be satisfied to live for less than a celestial life.

Providence

God is not only literally the Father of our spirits, but he has a providential concern for us and all of his works.

President John Taylor said:

. . . He governs this and other worlds, regulates all the systems and gives them their motions and revolutions; He preserves them in their various orbits, and governs them by unerring, unchangeable laws, as they traverse the immensity of space. In our world He gives day and night, summer and winter, seedtime and harvest; He adapts man, the beasts of the field, the fowls of the air and the fishes of the sea to their various climates and elements. He takes care of and provides for not only the hundreds of millions of the human family, but the myriads of beasts, fowls and fishes; He feeds and provides for them day by day, giving them their breakfast, dinner and supper; He takes care of the reptiles and other creeping things, and feeds the myriads of animalculae, which crowd earth, air and water. His hand is over all, and His providence sustains all. (*JD* 10: 260, October 10, 1863.)

In a similar vein President Brigham Young said:

. . . He is our Heavenly Father; He is also our God, and the Maker and upholder of all things in heaven and on earth. He sends forth His counsels and extends His providences to all living. He is the Supreme Controller of the universe. At His rebuke the sea is dried up, and the rivers become a wilderness. He measures the waters in the hollow of His hand, and meteth out heaven with a span, and comprehendeth the dust of the earth in a measure, and weigheth the mountains in scales, and the hills in a balance; the nations to Him are as a drop in a bucket, and He taketh up the isles as a very little thing; the hairs of our heads are numbered by Him, and not a sparrow falleth to the ground without our Father; and He knoweth every thought and intent of the hearts of all living, for He is everywhere present by the power of His Spirit — His minister the Holy Ghost. He is the Father of all, is above all, through all, and in you all; He knoweth all things pertaining to this earth, and He knows all things pertaining to millions of earths like this. (*Ibid.*, 11:41, January 8, 1865.)

God's Work

Consistent with the foregoing words of two latter-day prophets is the Lord's own declaration to Moses: "For behold, this is my work and my glory—to bring to pass the immortality and eternal life of man." (Moses 1:39.) Speaking generally, mankind has not been willing to receive God's will, and he has exercised great patience with those who have made covenant with him in the various dispensations, for even they, in large part, have not been constant. But even so, as President John Taylor said: "As a kind and beneficent father towards His children, He has been seeking from generation to generation to promote the welfare, the happiness, and the exaltation of the human family." (*JD* 24:125, April 8, 1883.)

Conclusion

It should be a source of incomparable joy to men to understand the following even in a very finite or limited way.

1. God himself was once as we are now.
2. God is now an exalted man.
3. God knows mortality from personal experience.
4. He has spoken to some of his prophets.
5. He has been seen by some of his prophets.

6. He is the most intelligent being known.
7. His knowledge and benevolence are supreme.
8. He is just.
9. He is merciful.
10. He organized the worlds.
11. He gave all kingdoms their respective laws.
12. He is literally the Father of the spirits of men.
13. He is not only our Father but also our God.
14. He has a providential and fatherly concern for men.
15. It is his work and glory to bring about the immortality and eternal life of man.
16. He wants us to be filled with joy.

Chapter II

JEHOVAH: SON AND REDEEMER

"Jehovah" is the anglicized form of the Hebrew name *Yahweh* or *Jahveh*. It means the *Self-existent One* or *The Eternal*. This name is essentially the same as that revealed to Moses when he was instructed to tell the children of Israel, "I Am hath sent me unto you." Identifying himself for Moses, the Lord declared his name to be "I Am That I Am." (Exodus 3:13-14.) In effect the Lord was saying to Moses that he is without beginning of days or end of years, that he is identical with existence, that he did not come to be nor will he cease to be. The connotation is essentially the same as another of his names used in the scriptures, *Alpha and Omega*, the first and the last, or the beginning and the end. Summarily, his names mean I am he who really is, or I am he who eternally exists.

The name by which he is most frequently called in the Christian world is Jesus Christ, "Jesus" meaning *Savior* (Matthew 1:21), and "Christ" meaning *Messiah*. (John 1:41.) The words "Savior" and "Messiah" are sometimes used along with other sacred titles such as the Only Begotten Son, Son of God, Son of Man, Emmanuel, the Anointed One, Redeemer, the Holy One of Israel, Lamb of God, Lamb without spot and without blemish, and Firstborn.

Each of these titles has its particular meaning, but in general these titles refer to two kinds of things:

(1) The relation of Jesus Christ to the Father and (2) The mission of Jesus Christ in behalf of mankind.

Jesus Is the Literal Son of God

Among the titles of the first kind perhaps the most prominent are the Only Begotten Son, Son of God, Son of Man, and Firstborn.

In "A Doctrinal Exposition by the First Presidency and the Twelve," dated June 30, 1916, is the following statement which clearly and emphatically sets forth the doctrine that Elohim is not only the Father of the spirits of all men, but that he is the Father of both the Spirit and the body of the Lord Jesus Christ.

Scriptures embodying the ordinary signification — literally that of Parent — are too numerous and specific to require citation. The purport of these scriptures is to the effect that God the Eternal Father, whom we designate by the exalted name-title "Elohim," is the literal Parent of our Lord and Savior Jesus Christ, and of the spirits of the human race. Elohim is the Father in every sense in which Jesus Christ is so designated, and distinctively He is the Father of spirits. Thus we read in the Epistle to the Hebrews: "Furthermore we have had fathers of our flesh which corrected us, and we gave them reverence: shall we not much rather be in subjection unto the Father of spirits, and live?" (Hebrews 12:9.) In view of this fact we are taught by Jesus Christ to pray: "Our Father which art in heaven, Hallowed be thy name."

. . . Jesus Christ is the Son of Elohim both as spiritual and bodily offspring; that is to say, Elohim is literally the Father of the spirit of Jesus Christ and also of the body in which Jesus Christ performed His mission in the flesh, and which body died on the cross and was afterward taken up by the process of resurrection, and is now the immortalized tabernacle of the eternal spirit of our Lord and Savior. (AF:466.)

President Joseph F. Smith, who was President of the Church at the time the above statement was issued, spoke on this subject in a conference of the Box Elder Stake conducted on December 19 and 20, 1914. A local newspaper reported the following:

President Smith stated that it is a perplexing thing to him why men persist in evading the simple truth in connection with the conception and birth of the Saviour. . . . He declared that God accomplishes all His purposes on natural principles and if man has been created in the exact image of God then God must be exactly like man in form and Mary the virgin, is the mother of Jesus while God the Eternal Father is the actual

father of Jesus just the same as earthly parents are the fathers
and mothers of their children. President Smith emphasized the
fact that God is the father of the Saviour, not the Holy Ghost
nor any other influence or spirit. The Saviour is in reality the
"only begotten of the Father" and God is actualy [sic] and
truly His father. (*The Box Elder News,* for Thursday, December 24, 1914, p. 2.)

Regarding the paternity of Jesus Christ President
Brigham Young declared:

When the time came that his First-born, the Savior, should
come into the world and take a tabernacle, the Father came himself and favored that Spirit with a tabernacle instead of letting
any other man do it. The Savior was begotten by the Father
and his Spirit, by the same Being who is the Father
of our spirits, and that is all the organic difference between
Jesus Christ and you and me. (*DBY*:50.)

The First Presidency of the Church in 1912, writing upon Jesus' Sonship to Elohim also makes reference
to the title, Firstborn. They wrote:

... It was our Father in Heaven who begat the spirit of him
who was the Firstborn of all spirits that come to this earth
and who was also his Father by the Virgin Mary, making him
"the Only Begotten in the flesh." Read Luke 1:26-35. Where
is Jesus called "the Only Begotten of the Holy Ghost"? He is
always singled out as "the Only Begotten of the Father." (John
14:3, 16-18, etc.) The Holy Ghost came upon Mary, her conception was under that influence, even of the spirit of life; our
Father in Heaven was the Father of the Son of Mary, to whom
the Savior prayed, as did our earthly father Adam. (Joseph
Fielding Smith, *Man: His Origin and Destiny* [Salt Lake City:
Deseret Book Co., 1954], p. 345.)

The Son of Man

The above statements account for Jesus' being
called the Only Begotten Son, the Son of God, and the
Firstborn, but why is he called Son of Man? Does
that refer to his having lived among men, or his having
inherited the capacity to die, from his maternal line?
No! This title, as the others mentioned, denotes his di-

vine origin, for "Man" in the title is only an abbrevi-
ation for one of the names of Elohim. "For, in the lan-
gage of Adam, Man of Holiness is his name, and the
name of his Only Begotten is the Son of Man, even
Jesus Christ. . . ." (Moses 6:57.)

Therefore, Jesus Christ is the Son of God, the Son
of an Exalted Man (Man of Holiness). But furthermore he is "the Firstborn of all spirits that come to this
earth" and is the Father's Only Begotten Son in the
flesh.

Some of the titles applied to the Lord Jesus Christ
which have to do primarily with his mission in behalf
of mankind are the following: the Anointed One, the
Redeemer, Savior, Messiah, Christ, Lamb of God, and
Lamb without spot and without blemish. All of these
titles connote, in one way or another, the great atonement.

The Atonement Revealed

From the days of Adam it was known among men
that the Son of God was to come to the earth and suffer
the atonement.

Adam was given commandments, which he taught
to his posterity, that he should worship the Lord and offer the *firstlings* of his flocks for an offering unto the
Lord. (Moses 5:5.)

And after many days an angel of the Lord appeared unto
Adam, saying: Why dost thou offer sacrifices unto the Lord?
And Adam said unto him: I know not, save the Lord commanded
me. And then the angel spake, saying: This thing is a similitude
of the sacrifice of the Only Begotten of the Father which is
full of grace and truth.

Wherefore, thou shalt do all that thou doest in the name of
the Son, and thou shalt repent and call upon God in the name
of the Son forevermore.

And in that day the Holy Ghost fell upon Adam, which
beareth record of the Father and the Son, saying: I am the
Only Begotten of the Father from the beginning, henceforth

and forever, that as thou hast fallen thou mayest be redeemed, and all mankind, even as many as will. (*Ibid.*, 5:6-9.)

The sacrifices offered by Adam and his posterity were in similitude of the great sacrifice which was to be made later by Elohim and his Son. For just as Adam and his descendants were to offer the *firstlings* of their flock, so Elohim was going to offer the *Firstborn* of his "flock" (his spirit children).

In a mighty vision Enoch was shown the unique mission of the Lord. Moses records:

And the Lord said unto Enoch: Look, and he looked and beheld the Son of Man lifted up on the cross, after the manner of men;

And he heard a loud voice; and the heavens were veiled; and all the creations of God mourned; and the earth groaned; and the rocks were rent; and the saints arose, and were crowned at the right hand of the Son of Man, with crowns of glory;

And as many of the spirits as were in prison came forth, and stood on the right hand of God; and the remainder were reserved in chains of darkness until the judgment of the great day.

And again Enoch wept and cried unto the Lord, saying: When shall the earth rest?

And it came to pass that Enoch saw the day of the coming of the Son of Man, in the last days, to dwell on the earth in righteousness for the space of a thousand years. (*Ibid.*, 7:55-58; 65.)

Noah taught his generation redemption through Jesus Christ. (*Ibid.*, 8:3-24.) Abraham was acquainted with Jesus' mission. (Abraham 3:22-28.) Joseph, the son of Jacob, knew of the Messiah's coming. (2 Nephi 3:5; 4:1-2.) Moses understood that the Only Begotten of the Father is the Savior. (Moses 1:6.)

Isaiah was shown many things, and part of his testimony is the following.

Therefore the Lord himself shall give you a sign; Behold, a virgin shall conceive, and bear a son, and shall call his name Immanuel. (Isaiah 7:14.)

For unto us a child is born, unto us a son is given: and the government shall be upon his shoulder: and his name shall be called Wonderful, Counsellor, The mighty God, the everlasting Father, The Prince of Peace. Of the increase of his government and peace there shall be no end, upon the throne of David, and upon his kingdom, to order it, and to establish it with judgment and with justice from henceforth even forever. The zeal of the Lord of hosts will perform this. (*Ibid.*, 9:6-7.)

Who hath believed our report? and to whom is the arm of the Lord revealed? For he shall grow up before him as a tender plant, and as a root out of a dry ground: he hath no form nor comeliness; and when we shall see him, there is no beauty that we should desire him. He is despised and rejected of men; a man of sorrows, and acquainted with grief: and we hid as it were our faces from him; he was despised, and we esteemed him not. Surely he hath borne our griefs, and carried our sorrows: yet we did esteem him stricken, smitten of God, and afflicted. But he was wounded for our transgressions, he was bruised for our iniquities: the chastisement of our peace was upon him; and with his stripes we are healed. All we like sheep have gone astray; we have turned every one to his own way; and the Lord hath laid on him the iniquity of us all. He was oppressed, and he was afflicted, yet he opened not his mouth: he is brought as a lamb to the slaughter, and as a sheep before her shearers is dumb, so he openeth not his mouth. He was taken from prison and from judgment: and who shall declare his generation? for he was cut off out of the land of the living: for the transgression of my people was he stricken. And he made his grave with the wicked, and with the rich in his death; because he had done no violence, neither was any deceit in his mouth. Yet it pleased the Lord to bruise him; he hath put him to grief: when thou shalt make his soul an offering for sin, he shall see his seed, he shall prolong his days, and the pleasure of the Lord shall prosper in his hand. He shall see of the travail of his soul, and shall be satisfied: by his knowledge shall my righteous servant justify many; for he shall bear their iniquities. Therefore will I divide him a portion with the great, and he shall divide the spoil with the strong; because he hath poured out his soul unto death: and he was numbered with the transgressors; and he bare the sin of many, and made intercession for the transgressors. (*Ibid.*, 53:1-12.)

Similarly, Nephi and other prophets among his people were shown the Lord's mission hundreds of years prior to his advent in Bethlehem; for example, Nephi said:

And it came to pass that the angel spake unto me again, saying: Look! And I looked and beheld the Lamb of God, that he was taken by the people; yea, the Son of the everlasting God was judged of the world; and I saw and bear record.

And I, Nephi, saw that he was lifted up upon the cross and slain for the sins of the world. (1 Nephi 11:32-33.)

The Birth of the Savior

When the time came for Jehovah to take upon himself a tabernacle of flesh and bones, the Angel Gabriel was sent from God to a virgin of Nazareth named Mary, and declared unto her:

Hail, thou that art highly favoured, the Lord is with thee: blessed art thou among women. And when she saw him, she was troubled at his saying, and cast in her mind what manner of salutation this should be. And the angel said unto her, Fear not, Mary: for thou hast found favour with God. And, behold, thou shalt conceive in thy womb, and bring forth a son, and shalt call his name Jesus. He shall be great, and shall be called the Son of the Highest: and the Lord God shall give unto him the throne of his father David: And he shall reign over the house of Jacob for ever; and of his kingdom there shall be no end. Then said Mary unto the angel, How shall this be, seeing I know not a man? And the angel answered and said unto her, The Holy Ghost shall come upon thee, and the power of the Highest shall overshadow thee: therefore also that holy thing which shall be born of thee, shall be called the Son of God. (Luke 1:28-35.)

When Jesus was born, an angel appeared to some shepherds of Judea and announced to them: "Fear not: for, behold, I bring you good tidings of great joy, which shall be to all people. For unto you is born this day in the city of David, a Saviour, which is Christ the Lord." (*Ibid.*, 2:10-11.)

During Jesus' ministry he tried in various ways to prepare his disciples for his own death, but they did not seem to understand.

Jesus Taught the Atonement

Matthew records the great conversation at Caesarea Philippi in which Peter bore solemn testimony of Jesus' divinity, and the Lord told him it was by the power of revelation and spoke of the keys of the priesthood, and then Matthew continues:

From that time forth began Jesus to shew unto his disciples, how that he must go unto Jerusalem, and suffer many things of the elders and chief priests and scribes, and be killed, and be raised again the third day. Then Peter took him, and began to rebuke him, saying, Be it far from thee, Lord: this shall not be unto thee. But he turned, and said unto Peter, Get thee behind me, Satan: thou art an offense unto me: for thou savourest not the things that be of God, but those that be of man. (Matthew 16:21-23.)

And again, a short time thereafter, while he and the twelve were still in Galilee he said:

... The Son of man shall be betrayed into the hands of men: And they shall kill him, and the third day he shall be raised again. And they were exceeding sorry. (*Ibid.*, 17:22-23.)

Again, a short time prior to the passion week the Lord predicted the imminence of his suffering:

And they were in the way going up to Jerusalem; and Jesus went before them: and they were amazed; and as they followed, they were afraid. And he took again the twelve, and began to tell them what things should happen unto him. Saying, Behold, we go up to Jerusalem; and the Son of man shall be delivered unto the chief priests, and unto the scribes; and they shall condemn him to death, and shall deliver him to the Gentiles: And they shall mock him, and shall scourge him, and shall spit upon him, and shall kill him; and the third day he shall rise again. (Mark 10:32-34.)

On the third day of the passion week certain Greeks who were at the feast came to the disciples and requested to see Jesus.

And Jesus answered them, saying, The hour is come, that the Son of man should be glorified. Verily, verily, I say unto you, Except a corn of wheat fall into the ground and die, it abideth alone: but if it die, it bringeth forth much fruit. He that loveth his life shall lose it; and he that hateth his life in this world shall keep it unto life eternal. If any man serve me, let him follow me; and where I am, there shall also my servant be: if any man serve me, him will my Father honour. Now is my soul troubled; and what shall I say? Father, save me from this hour: but for this cause came I unto this hour. Father, glorify thy name. Then came there a voice from heaven, saying, I have both glorified it, and will glorify it again. The people therefore, that stood by, and heard it, said that it thundered: others said, An angel spake to him. Jesus answered and said, This voice came not because of me, but for your sakes. Now is the judgment of this world: now shall the prince of this world be cast out. And I, if I be lifted up from the earth, will draw all men unto me. This he said, signifying what death he should die. The people answered him, We have heard out of the law that Christ abideth for ever: and how sayest thou, The Son of man must be lifted up? who is this Son of man? Then Jesus said unto them, Yet a little while is the light with you. Walk while ye have the light, lest darkness come upon you: for he that walketh in darkness knoweth not whither he goeth. While ye have light, believe in the light, that ye may be the children of light. These things spake Jesus, and departed, and did hide himself from them. (John 12:23-36.)

The Atonement

Finally, in the evening of the fifth day of passion week, after celebrating the passover, having his last supper, washing the disciples' feet, instituting the ordinance of the Sacrament, giving his last great discourses, and offering his prayer for his disciples and prophesying concerning them, he retired to the Garden of Gethsemane. He said to most of the twelve: "Sit ye here, while I go and pray yonder." He took Peter, James,

and John with him, "Then saith he unto them, My soul
is exceeding sorrowful, even unto death: tarry ye here,
and watch with me. And he went a little farther, and
fell on his face, and prayed, saying, O my Father, if it
be possible, let this cup pass from me: nevertheless not
as I will, but as thou wilt." (Matthew 26:36-39.)

And there appeared an angel unto him from heaven,
strengthening him. And being in an agony he prayed more
earnestly: and his sweat was as it were great drops of blood
falling down to the ground. (Luke 22:43-44.)

Then Jesus rose, went to his disciples, and found
them asleep. He retired again and prayed a second time
as he had before. He went to his disciples again and
found them still asleep. A third time he retired and
prayed to his Father as he had done before. (See *ibid.*,
26:40-46.)

Sometimes it is not recognized that Jesus' suffering
in the Garden was a fundamental part of his atoning
sacrifice. However, Luke reports that the Lord's agony
in the Garden was so intense that "his sweat was as it
were great drops of blood falling down to the ground."

President Joseph Fielding Smith gives us insight
into this great event. He says:

We speak of the passion of Jesus Christ. A great many
people have an idea that when he was on the cross, and nails were
driven into his hands and feet, that was his great suffering. His
great suffering was before he ever was placed upon the cross.
It was in the Garden of Gethsemane that the blood oozed from
the pores of his body: "which suffering caused myself, even
God, the greatest of all, to tremble because of pain, and to
bleed at every pore, and to suffer both body and spirit — and
would that I might not drink the bitter cup, and shrink." (D&C
19:18.)

That was not when he was on the cross; that was in the
garden. That is where he bled from every pore in his body.

Now I cannot comprehend that pain. I have suffered pain,
you have suffered pain, and sometimes it has been quite severe;

but I cannot comprehend pain, which is *mental anguish more than physical*, that would cause the blood, like sweat, to come out upon the body. It was something terrible, something terrific; so we can understand why he would cry unto his Father: "If it be possible, let this cup pass from me: nevertheless not as I will, but as thou wilt." (*DS* I:130.)

After the betrayal by Judas Iscariot the Lord was taken to Annas, Caiaphas, the Sanhedrin, Pilate, Herod, and Pilate again and all the while suffering a host of humiliations, indignities, and physical pains.

Finally, at the place called Calvary, he was crucified between two malefactors. Suffering the anguish of the cross he said, "It is finished," "bowed his head, and gave up the ghost." (John 19:30.)

We cannot conceive of the suffering he experienced in crucifixion. Serious contemplation of such a death almost makes one ill. But although he was a divine Being, bearing the sins of the world in his suffering, thousands of mortals were executed by crucifixion. This all the more emphasizes the anguish he suffered in the Garden, which was an altogether unique experience.

All men know they must eventually die the temporal death, but how must it have been for the great Jehovah to know both prior to his mortal birth and throughout his mortal years that he would eventually suffer for the sins of all mankind. We sometimes quail at the thought of having to suffer only for our own sins. Try to imagine anticipating having to suffer for the sins of all mankind.

Love the Lord thy God with all thy heart, soul, mind, and strength, and love thy neighbor as thyself are meaningful to a point beyond human expression when contemplated with the infinite love, mercy, humility, patience, forbearance, etc., which were manifested by the Lord Jesus Christ in his suffering for the sins of the world.

"Sins of the world" connotes all sins. But this may sometimes seem a little remote or impersonal. Even to say "our sins" is a bit general. We need to come to grips with the fact that he suffered for *my sins* and *your sins*.

Conclusion

It should grieve our souls, *yours* and *mine*, to think of his suffering, but it should give us unspeakable joy to know that he loves us so much that he was willing to give himself for us as he did.

Chapter III

BLESSINGS THROUGH THE ATONEMENT

There are many blessings which have already come to mankind and others which will be theirs because of the atonement of the Lord Jesus Christ. One does not need to contemplate upon the matter very long until he realizes what a vast network of blessings are his due to the Lord's being the Redeemer.

Here we will discuss only five generic or very general blessings which are results of the atonement. They are: (1) Resurrection, (2) Forgiveness of sins, (3) Salvation of those who die in their childhood, (4) Salvation of those who die without the law, and (5) Freedom-captivity alternatives.

Resurrection

Some of the best-known words of the Lord regarding his power in the resurrection are recorded in the Gospel of John. They are:

I am the resurrection and the life: he that believeth in me, though he were dead, yet shall he live. (John 11:25.)

Therefore doth my Father love me, because I lay down my life, that I might take it again.

No man taketh it from me, but I lay it down of myself. I have power to lay it down, and I have power to take it again. This commandment have I received of my Father. (*Ibid.*, 10: 17-18.)

And I, if I be lifted up from the earth, will draw all men unto me.

This he said, signifying what death he should die. (*Ibid.*, 12:32-33.)

No man can come to me, except the Father which hath sent me draw him: and I will raise him up at the last day. (*Ibid.*, 6:44.)

For I came down from heaven, not to do mine own will, but the will of him that sent me.

And this is the Father's will which hath sent me, that of all which he hath given me I should lose nothing, but should raise it up again at the last day.

And this is the will of him that sent me, that every one which seeth the Son, and believeth on him, may have everlasting life: and I will raise him up at the last day. (*Ibid.*, 6:38-40.)

Amulek, the Book of Mormon prophet, in a remarkable passage, explains the relation of the resurrection to the Christ very clearly. He says:

Now, there is a death which is called a temporal death; and the death of Christ shall loose the bands of this temporal death, that all shall be raised from this temporal death.

The spirit and the body shall be reunited again in its perfect form; both limb and joint shall be restored to its proper frame, even as we now are at this time; and we shall be brought to stand before God, knowing even as we know now, and have a bright recollection of all our guilt.

Now, this restoration shall come to all, both old and young, both bond and free, both male and female, both the wicked and the righteous; and even there shall not so much as a hair of their heads be lost; but every thing shall be restored to its perfect frame, as it is now, or in the body, and shall be brought and be arraigned before the bar of Christ the Son, and God the Father, and the Holy Spirit, which is one Eternal God, to be judged according to their works, whether they be good or whether they be evil.

Now, behold, I have spoken unto you concerning the death of the mortal body, and also concerning the resurrection of the mortal body. I say unto you that this mortal body is raised to an immortal body, that is from death, even from the first death unto life, that they can die no more; their spirits uniting with their bodies, never to be divided; thus the whole becoming spiritual and immortal, that they can no more see corruption. (Alma 11:42-45.)

Abinadi succinctly gives his witness of resurrection through Jesus Christ in the following words:

And if Christ had not risen from the dead, or have broken the bands of death that the grave should have no victory, and that death should have no sting, there could have been no resurrection.

But there is a resurrection, therefore the grave hath no victory, and the sting of death is swallowed up in Christ. (Mosiah 16:7-8.)

Forgiveness of Sins

Another great blessing available to man which can come only through the Lord Jesus Christ is forgiveness of sins. Just as all mankind are mortal and have to die, similarly all mankind have committed sins and need to obtain forgiveness.

On one occasion when Jesus was talking to the ancient Palestinian Jews, as recorded in the Gospel of John, he was emphatic that it was only through *accepting* him that one can obtain a forgiveness of sins. He said:

I said therefore unto you, that ye shall die in your sins: for if ye believe not that I am he, ye shall die in your sins. (John 8:24.)

The prophets speak of man's being out of the presence of God as spiritual death. Therefore, in addition to man's having to die the temporal death, or death of the body, all mankind as mortals experience the first spiritual death. In order to overcome the first spiritual death, obtain a forgiveness of sins, and avoid the second spiritual death, that of being eternally separated from God's presence, we must turn to Christ the Redeemer and repent of our sins.

Samuel the Lamanite taught this impressively, prophesying of the Lord's coming, when he said:

For behold, he surely must die that salvation may come; yea, it behooveth him and becometh expedient that he dieth, to bring to pass the resurrection of the dead, that thereby men may be brought into the presence of the Lord.

Yea, behold, this death bringeth to pass the resurrection, and redeemeth all mankind from the first death — that spiritual death; for all mankind, by the fall of Adam being cut off from the presence of the Lord, are considered as dead, both as to things temporal and to things spiritual.

But behold, the resurrection of Christ redeemeth mankind, yea, even all mankind, and bringeth them back into the presence of the Lord.

Yea, and it bringeth to pass the condition of repentance, that whosoever repenteth the same is not hewn down and cast into the fire; but whosoever repenteth not is hewn down and cast into the fire; and there cometh upon them again a spiritual death, yea, a second death, for they are cut off again as to things pertaining to righteousness. (Helaman 14:15-18.)

When the resurrected Lord visited the Nephites he identified himself as he who was to come and he through whom forgiveness of sins comes. He declared:

Behold, I am Jesus Christ, whom the prophets testified shall come into the world.

And behold, I am the light and the life of the world; and I have drunk out of that bitter cup which the Father hath given me, and have glorified the Father in taking upon me the sins of the world, in the which I have suffered the will of the Father in all things from the beginning.

When the Nephites heard these words the whole multitude fell to the earth and then the Lord said:

Arise and come forth unto me, that ye may thrust your hands into my side, and also that ye may feel the prints of the nails in my hands and in my feet, that ye may know that I am the God of Israel, and the God of the whole earth, and have been slain for the sins of the world. (3 Nephi 11:10-11, 14.)

In our own dispensation, in a revelation to the Prophet Joseph Smith, the Lord identified himself as the Redeemer as follows:

I am Jesus Christ, the Son of God, who was crucified for the sins of the world, even as many as will believe on my name, that they may become the sons of God, even one in me as I am one in the Father, as the Father is one in me, that we may be one. (D&C 35:2.)

We need to become as enthusiastic in this knowledge as was Nephi, the son of Lehi. He said:

And we talk of Christ, we rejoice in Christ, we preach of Christ, we prophesy of Christ, and we write according to our prophesies, *that our children may know to what source they may look for a remission of sins.* (2 Nephi 25-26. Italics ours.)

Salvation for Those Who Die in Childhood

A third great blessing which comes to mankind by virtue of the atonement of the Lord is the salvation of children who die before they reach the age of accountability.

In a modern revelation through the Prophet Joseph Smith, the Lord said:

But, behold, I say unto you, that little children are redeemed from the foundation of the world through mine Only Begotten; Wherefore, they cannot sin, for power is not given unto Satan to tempt little children, until they begin to become accountable before me . . . (D&C 29:46-47.)

King Benjamin, in his remarkable sermon, speaks of the effect of the atonement upon those who die as children. He says:

And even if it were possible that little children could sin they could not be saved; but I say unto you they are blessed; for behold, as in Adam, or by nature, they fall, even so the blood of Christ atoneth for their sins.

And moreover, I say unto you that there shall be no other name given nor any other way nor means whereby salvation can come unto the children of men, only in and through the name of Christ, the Lord Omnipotent.

For behold he judgeth, and his judgment is just; and the infant perisheth not that dieth in his infancy; but men drink damnation to their own souls except they humble themselves and become as little children, and believe that salvation was, and is, and is to come, in and through the atoning blood of Christ, the Lord Omnipotent.

For the natural man is an enemy to God, and has been from the fall of Adam, and will be, forever and ever, unless he yields to the enticings of the Holy Spirit, and putteth off the natural man and becometh a saint through the atonement of Christ the Lord, and becometh as a child, submissive, meek, humble, patient, full of love, willing to submit to all things which the Lord seeth fit to inflict upon him, even as a child doth submit to his father.

And moreover, I say unto you, that the time shall come when the knowledge of a Savior shall spread throughout every nation, kindred, tongue, and people.

And behold, when that time cometh, none shall be found blameless before God, except it be little children, only through repentance and faith on the name of the Lord God Omnipotent. (Mosiah 3:16-21.)

Perhaps there are no more forceful words from the prophets regarding the redemption of children than those contained in an epistle of Mormon to his son Moroni. Mormon declares:

And the word of the Lord came to me by the power of the Holy Ghost, saying:

Listen to the words of Christ, your Redeemer, your Lord and your God. Behold, I came into the world not to call the righteous but sinners to repentance; the whole need no physician, but they that are sick; wherefore, little children are whole, for they are not capable of committing sin; wherefore the curse of Adam is taken from them in me, that it hath no power over them; and the law of circumcision is done away in me.

And after this manner did the Holy Ghost manifest the word of God unto me; wherefore, my beloved son, I know that it is solemn mockery before God, that ye should baptize little children.

Behold I say unto you that this thing shall ye teach — repentance and baptism unto those who are accountable and capable of committing sin; yea, teach parents that they must repent and be baptized, and humble themselves as their little children, and they shall all be saved with their little children.

And their little children need no repentance, neither baptism. Behold, baptism is unto repentance to the fulfilling the commandments unto the remission of sins.

But little children are alive in Christ, even from the foundation of the world . . . .

Little children cannot repent; wherefore, it is awful wickedness to deny the pure mercies of God unto them, for they are all alive in him because of his mercy.

And he that saith that little children need baptism denieth the mercies of Christ, and setteth at naught the atonement of him and the power of his redemption.

Wo unto such, for they are in danger of death, hell, and an endless torment. I speak it boldly; God hath commanded me. Listen unto them and give heed, or they stand against you at the judgment-seat of Christ. (Moroni 8:7-12, 19-21.)

On Thursday, January 21, 1836, after recording an account of a vision of the celestial kingdom and a revelation from the Lord, Joseph Smith states:

And I also beheld that all children who die before they arrive at the years of accountability, are saved in the celestial kingdom of heaven. (*DHC* II:381.)

President Joseph Fielding Smith, discussing this matter, says:

Little children who die before they reach the years of accountability will automatically inherit the celestial kingdom, but not the exaltation in that kingdom *until* they have complied with all the requirements of exaltation.

For instance:

The crowning glory is marriage and this ordinance would have to be performed in their behalf *before* they could inherit the fulness of that kingdom. The Lord is just with all his children, and little children who die will not be penalized as the Catholic Church penalizes them, simply because they happen to die. *The Lord will grant unto these children the privilege of all the sealing blessings which pertain to the exaltation.*

We were all mature spirits before we were born, and the bodies of little children will grow after the resurrection to the full stature of the spirit, and *all the blessings will be theirs through their obedience, the same as if they had lived to maturity and received them on the earth.* (*DS* II:54.)

Regarding Those Who Die Not Knowing the Law

Still another blessing which comes to a vast multitude of mankind through the atonement wrought by the great Jehovah, is the redemption of those who do not know the law as mortals and have no opportunity to either accept it or reject it while in the flesh.

Paul writes of this to the Romans in saying: "For there is no respect of persons with God. For as many as have sinned without law shall also perish without law: and as many as have sinned in the law shall be judged by the law." (Romans 2:11-12.)

Jacob, the brother of Nephi and the son of Lehi, has provided us with the following words which express this aspect of the Lord's atoning sacrifice very clearly:

Wherefore, he has given a law; and where there is no law given there is no punishment; and where there is no punishment there is no condemnation; and where there is no condemnation the mercies of the Holy One of Israel have claim upon them, because of the atonement; for they are delivered by the power of him.

For the atonement satisfieth the demands of his justice upon all those who have not the law given to them, that they are delivered from that awful monster, death and hell, and the devil, and the lake of fire and brimstone, which is endless torment; and they are restored to that God who gave them breath, which is the Holy One of Israel.

But wo unto him that has the law given, yea, that has all the commandments of God, like unto us, and that transgresseth them, and that wasteth the days of his probation, for awful is his state! (2 Nephi 9:25-27.)

In a revelation of this dispensation the Lord, speaking concerning the last days, said through his prophet, Joseph Smith:

And then shall the heathen nations be redeemed, and they that knew no law shall have part in the first resurrection; and it shall be tolerable for them. (D&C 45:54.)

The Freedom-Captivity Alternatives

The last great blessing we shall mention here which comes to mankind as a result of the atonement of the Lord Jesus Christ is the freedom to choose between the freedom-captivity, eternal life-death, alternatives.

In the state of pre-mortal existence Lucifer attempted to take away the agency of man. The account of this event in the book of Moses reads as follows:

Wherefore, because that Satan rebelled against me, and sought to destroy the agency of man, which I, the Lord God, had given him, and also, that I should give unto him mine own power; by the power of mine Only Begotten, I caused that he should be cast down;

And he became Satan, yea even the devil, the father of all lies, to deceive and to blind men, and to lead them captive at his will, even as many as would not hearken unto my voice. (Moses 4:3-4.)

When Adam and Eve were in the garden of Eden, the devil beguiled Eve and set off a chain of events which caused the fall of man. This event brought both sin and death into the world. Mankind became what the Book of Mormon prophets call natural man, an enemy to God. (See chapter on the Holy Ghost.) Natural man was a captive of the devil. As a captive of the devil he really had no choice. Whatever he would do, whether it might be termed "good" or "evil," he was within the power of Satan, and there were no *real* alternatives available to him. In effect, it would appear that as a consequence of the fall, Lucifer had accomplished his purpose in trying to thwart Elohim's plan inasmuch as he had for all intents destroyed the agency of man.

However, God in his wisdom prepared the means by which man's agency should not be destroyed, for as Lehi explained to his sons:

And the Messiah cometh in the fulness of time, that he may redeem the children of men from the fall. And because that they are redeemed from the fall they have become free forever, knowing good from evil; to act for themselves and not to be acted upon, save it be by the punishment of the law at the great and last day, according to the commandments which God hath given.

Wherefore, men are free according to the flesh; and all things are given them which are expedient unto man. And they are free to choose liberty and eternal life, through the great mediation of all men, or to choose captivity and death, according to the captivity and power of the devil; for he seeketh that all men might be miserable like unto himself. (2 Nephi 2:26-27.)

The Savior's coming made it possible that mankind could make *real* choices, and exercise *real* agency, and by choosing the way of the Lord man could attain liberty and eternal life. Our precious right to make genuine choices is another blessing from our Redeemer.

Necessity of the Atonement

The necessity of the atonement has been revealed from time to time even from the beginning; for example, the Lord said to Adam:

Therefore I give unto you a commandment, to teach things freely unto your children, saying:

That by reason of transgression cometh the fall, which fall bringeth death, and inasmuch as ye were born into the world by water, and blood, and the spirit, which I have made, and so became of dust a living soul, even so ye must be born again into the kingdom of heaven, of water, and of the Spirit, and be cleansed by blood, even the blood of mine Only Begotten; that ye might be sanctified from all sin, and enjoy the words of eternal life in this world, and eternal life in the world to come, even immortal glory;

For by the water ye keep the commandment; by the Spirit ye are justified, and by the blood ye are sanctified;

Therefore it is given to abide in you; the record of heaven; the Comforter; the peaceable things of immortal glory; the truth of all things; that which quickeneth all things, which maketh alive all things; that which knoweth all things, and hath all power, according to wisdom, mercy, truth, justice, and judgment.

And now, behold, I say unto you: This is the plan of salvation unto all men, through the blood of mine Only Begotten, who shall come in the meridian of time. (Moses 6:58-62.)

From the time of Adam until the Lord came there were burnt offerings and sacrifices. The blood sacrifices were atonements for sin. However, they were all in the similitude of the great anticipated atonement of the Son of God and were not efficacious in and of themselves but were dependent upon his sacrifice for their validity and power. For as King Benjamin of Zarahemla declared: "the law of Moses availeth nothing except it were through the atonement of his blood." (Mosiah 3:15.)

Aaron, the son of Mosiah the younger, said: "There could be no redemption for mankind save it were through the death and sufferings of Christ, and the atonement of his blood." (Alma 21:9.)

One of the most comprehensive scriptural statements concerning the necessity of the atonement of the Christ is the following testimony of Amulek:

And now, behold, I will testify unto you of myself that these things are true. Behold, I say unto you, that I do know that Christ shall come among the children of men, to take upon him the transgressions of his people, and that he shall atone for the sins of the world; for the Lord God hath spoken it.

For it is expedient that an atonement should be made; for according to the great plan of the Eternal God there must be an atonement made, or else all mankind must unavoidably perish; yea, all are hardened; yea, all are fallen and are lost, and must perish except it be through the atonement which it is expedient should be made.

For it is expedient that there should be a great and last sacrifice; yea, not a sacrifice of man, neither of beast, neither of any manner of fowl; for it shall not be a human sacrifice; but it must be an infinite and eternal sacrifice.

Now there is not any man that can sacrifice his own blood which will atone for the sins of another. Now, if a man murdereth, behold will our law, which is just, take the life of his brother? I say unto you, Nay.

But the law requireth the life of him who hath murdered; therefore there can be nothing which is short of an infinite atonement which will suffice for the sins of the world.

Therefore, it is expedient that there should be a great and last sacrifice; and then shall there be, or it is expedient there should be, a stop to the shedding of blood, then shall the law of Moses be fulfilled; yea, it shall be all fulfilled, every jot and tittle, and none shall have passed away.

And behold, this is the whole meaning of the law, every whit pointing to that great and last sacrifice; and that great and last sacrifice will be the Son of God, yea, infinite and eternal.

And thus he shall bring salvation to all those who shall believe on his name; this being the intent of this last sacrifice, to bring about the bowels of mercy, which overpowereth justice, and bringeth about means unto men that they may have faith unto repentance.

And thus mercy can satisfy the demands of justice, and encircles them in the arms of safety, while he that exercises no faith unto repentance is exposed to the whole law of the demands of justice; therefore only unto him that has faith unto repentance is brought about the great and eternal plan of redemption. (*Ibid.*, 34:8-16.)

Consequences Had There Been No Atonement

Men seldom, if ever, take the time to consider what the consequences for mankind would have been had there been no atonement by the Lord. Obviously, none of the blessings discussed here would have belonged to man had it not been for the atonement. But there is a much more impressive way of stating what would have been man's lot without the atonement. Jacob, the brother of Nephi, understood those horrible consequences well. He said:

For as death hath passed upon all men, to fulfil the merciful plan of the great Creator, there must needs be a power of resurrection, and the resurrection must needs come unto man by reason of the fall; and the fall came by reason of transgression; and because man became fallen they were cut off from the presence of the Lord.

Wherefore, it must needs be an infinite atonement — save it should be an infinite atonement this corruption could not put on incorruption. Wherefore, the first judgment which came upon man must needs have remained to an endless duration. And if so, this flesh must have laid down to rot and to crumble to its mother earth, to rise no more.

O the wisdom of God, his mercy and grace! For behold, if the flesh should rise no more our spirits must become subject to that angel who fell from before the presence of the Eternal God, and became the devil, to rise no more.

And our spirits must have become like unto him, and we become devils, angels to a devil, to be shut out from the presence of our God, and to remain with the father of lies, in misery, like unto himself; yea, to that being who beguiled our first parents, who transformeth himself nigh unto an angel of light, and stirreth up the children of men unto secret combinations of murder and all manner of secret works of darkness.

O how great the goodness of our God, who prepareth a way for our escape from the grasp of this awful monster; yea, that monster, death and hell, which I call the death of the body, and also the death of the spirit. (2 Nephi 9:6-10.)

Conclusion

As one enjoys the spirit and begins to understand in a limited measure what great things the Lord has done and does for him, he should come to realize how much the Lord loves mankind and gain some insight into the significance of these words of the Christ, "Greater love hath no man than this, that a man lay down his life for his friends." (John 15:13.)

When one begins to comprehend what great things the Redeemer has done for him, he cannot help humbly acknowledging that at best he is an unprofitable servant. His heart is caused to cry out as did King Benjamin's people: "O have mercy, and apply the atoning blood of Christ that we may receive forgiveness of our sins, and our hearts may be purified; for we believe in Jesus Christ, the Son. . . ." (Mosiah 4:2.)

One should also never forget that as Jesus bade his disciples to keep his commandments and love one another, he declared: "These things have I spoken unto you, that my joy might remain in you, and that your joy might be full." (John 15:11.)

Jesus did and does his work that your joy might be full.

Chapter IV

THE ROLES OF JESUS THE CHRIST

In the previous two chapters we have discussed some of the names and titles by which Jesus is known and some of the great blessings which come to man through his atoning sacrifice. But as fundamental and important as the atonement is, there are other very significant aspects to the Lord's work; for example, what was his status and role prior to the earth's existence? What did he have to do with the earth's coming into being? What did he have to do with mortals prior to his birth to Mary? What missionary labors did he perform other than those among the people in Palestine? What has he done for mortals since that time? What great work still lies ahead of the Lord? This chapter will treat these questions.

Jesus in the Council in Heaven

Among the names and titles discussed earlier is the Firstborn. As was indicated there, this name refers to Jesus' being the Firstborn of all the spirit children of Elohim who have or will come to live on this earth. As the Firstborn he was associated with the Father from the "beginning." In one revelation Jesus is identified as "my Beloved Son, which was my Beloved and Chosen from the beginning. . . ." (Moses 4:2.)

In the great council in heaven when all who have come to this earth were still in the pre-mortal estate as spirit beings only, it was Jehovah, the pre-existent Jesus, who sustained the plan of choice or agency in opposition to that of force. In a revelation to Moses the Lord spake saying:

That Satan, whom thou hast commanded in the name of mine Only Begotten, is the same which was from the beginning, and he came before me saying — Behold, here am I, send me, I will be thy son, and I will redeem all mankind, that one soul shall not be lost, and surely I will do it; wherefore give me thine honor.

But, behold, my Beloved Son, which was my Beloved and Chosen from the beginning, said unto me — Father, thy will be done, and the glory be thine forever.

Wherefore, because that Satan rebelled against me, and sought to destroy the agency of man, which I, the Lord God, had given him, and also, that I should give unto him mine own power; by the power of mine Only Begotten, I caused that he should be cast down; . . . (Moses 4:1-3.)

This passage clearly reveals that the Lord, Jehovah, was in complete accord with Elohim and that it was his desire that Elohim's will be done. Many times in Jesus' ministry among mortals, as recorded by John particularly, the Lord announced that he came not to do his own will but the will of the Father; for example:

My meat is to do the will of him that sent me, and to finish his work. (John 4:34.)

I can of mine own self do nothing: as I hear, I judge: and my judgment is just; because I seek not mine own will, but the will of the Father which hath sent me. (*Ibid.*, 5:30.)

But I have greater witness than that of John: for the works which the Father hath given me to finish, the same works that I do, bear witness of me, that the Father hath sent me. (*Ibid.*, 5:36.)

This is the work of God, that ye believe on him whom he hath sent. (*Ibid.*, 6:29.)

It seems clear from these passages that what we commonly call the plan of salvation or the gospel of Jesus Christ is the will of the Father, Elohim, and that in opposition to Lucifer, who proposed a plan antagonistic to God's will and the welfare of man, Jehovah arose in defense of the will of his Father and in the interest of his Father's other spirit children. (See also

President John Taylor's *The Mediation and Atonement*, pp. 93-94.)

Jesus Is the Creator

As a part of the great council already mentioned, according to a revelation given to Abraham, the creation of the earth and its purpose was discussed. Abraham records:

> And there stood one among them that was like unto God, and he said unto those who were with him: We will go down, for there is space there, and we will take of these materials, and we will make an earth whereon these may dwell;
>
> And we will prove them herewith, to see if they will do all things whatsoever the Lord their God shall command them;
>
> And they who keep their first estate shall be added upon; and they who keep not their first estate shall not have glory in the same kingdom with those who keep their first estate; and they who keep their second estate shall have glory added upon their heads for ever and ever. (Abraham 3:24-26.)

When the time came for the earth to be created or organized, the Lord said: "Let us go down. And they went down at the beginning, and they, that is the Gods, organized and formed the heavens and the earth." (*Ibid.*, 4:1.) Jehovah was the principal figure in the creation. John says:

> In the beginning was the Word, and the Word was with God, and the Word was God.
>
> The same was in the beginning with God.
>
> All things were made by him; and without him was not any thing made that was made.
>
> And the Word was made flesh, and dwelt among us, (and we beheld his glory, the glory as of the only begotten of the Father,) full of grace and truth. (John 1:1-3, 14.)

In writing to the Ephesians Paul says of God, he "created all things by Jesus Christ." (Ephesians 3:9.) In writing to the Hebrews he said: "God, who at sundry times and in divers manners spake in time past unto the fathers by the prophets, Hath in these last days spoken unto us by his Son, whom he hath appointed heir of all things, by whom also he made the worlds." (Hebrews 1:1-2.)

The Book of Mormon prophets understood very well that Jesus was the Creator. Jacob, the son of Lehi and brother of Nephi, said: "For it behooveth the great Creator that he suffereth himself to become subject unto man in the flesh, and die for all men, that all men might become subject unto him." (2 Nephi 9:5.)

King Benjamin, in his great discourse, prophesying of the Lord's coming, said: "And he shall be called Jesus Christ, the Son of God, the Father of heaven and earth, the Creator of all things from the beginning; and his mother shall be called Mary." (Mosiah 3:8. See also Helaman 14:12.)

When the Lord appeared to the Nephites he identified himself in unequivocal language as follows:

Behold, I am Jesus Christ the Son of God. I created the heavens and the earth, and all things that in them are. I was with the Father from the beginning. I am in the Father, and the Father in me; and in me hath the Father glorified his name. (3 Nephi 9:15.)

In similar words the Lord revealed himself to the Prophet Joseph Smith. For example, in a revelation to David Whitmer recorded in Section 38 of the Doctrine and Covenants, the Lord said:

Thus saith the Lord your God, even Jesus Christ, the Great I Am, Alpha and Omega, the beginning and the end, the same which looked upon the wide expanse of eternity, and all the seraphic hosts of heaven, before the world was made;

The same which knoweth all things, for all things are present before mine eyes;

I am the same which spake, and the world was made, and all things came by me. (D&C 38:1-3.)

One of the greatest testimonies of this kind is that of Joseph Smith and Sidney Rigdon recorded in the Prophet's account of their vision of the three degrees of glory. Joseph Smith declares:

> And now, after the many testimonies which have been given of him, this is the testimony, last of all, which we give of him: That he lives!
>
> For we saw him, even on the right hand of God; and we heard the voice bearing record that he is the Only Begotten of the Father—
>
> That by him, and through him, and of him, the worlds are and were created, and the inhabitants thereof are begotten sons and daughters unto God. (*Ibid.*, 76:22-24.)

Jesus Is the Lawgiver

After Jehovah had created the world and placed man upon it and man had fallen, it was he who gave instructions to the antediluvian patriarchs. In this dispensation the Lord has given us an account of one of his early ancient appearances among the patriarchs.

> Three years previous to the death of Adam, he called Seth, Enos, Cainan, Mahalaleel, Jared, Enoch, and Methuselah, who were all high priests, with the residue of his posterity who were righteous, into the valley of Adam-ondi-Ahman, and there bestowed upon them his last blessing.
>
> And the Lord appeared unto them, and they rose up and blessed Adam, and called him Michael, the prince, the archangel.
>
> And the Lord administered comfort unto Adam, and said unto him: I have set thee to be at the head; a multitude of nations shall come of thee, and thou art a prince over them forever.
>
> And Adam stood up in the midst of the congregation; and, notwithstanding he was bowed down with age, being full of the Holy Ghost, predicted whatsoever should befall his posterity unto the latest generation. (*Ibid.*, 107:53-56.)

Identifying himself as the one who so established Adam, in another modern revelation the Lord says:

> That you may come up unto the crown prepared for you, and be made rulers over many kingdoms, saith the Lord God,

the Holy One of Zion, who hath established the foundations of
Adam-ondi-Ahman;

Who hath appointed Michael your prince, and established
his feet, and set him upon high, and given unto him the keys of
salvation under the counsel and direction of the Holy One, who
is without beginning of days or end of life.

The Lord continues by saying: Wherefore, do the things
which I have commanded you, saith your Redeemer, even the
Son Ahman, who prepareth all things before he taketh you.
(*Ibid.*, 78:15-16, 20.)

When the Lord made the gospel and priesthood
covenant with Abraham, again it was Jehovah. Part of
that covenant follows:

My name is Jehovah, and I know the end from the beginning;
therefore my hand shall be over thee.

And I will make of thee a great nation, and I will bless thee
above measure, and make thy name great among all nations,
and thou shalt be a blessing unto thy seed after thee, that in
their hands they shall bear this ministry and Priesthood unto
all nations. (Abraham 2:8-9.)

Perhaps of all the scriptures which identify Jesus
Christ as the Jehovah of the Old Testament period of
man's history there is none which is more to the point
than the words of the Redeemer himself when he was
among the Nephites giving them instructions about the
law of Moses. He said:

Behold, I say unto you that the law is fulfilled that was
given unto Moses.

Behold, I am he that gave the law, and I am he who covenanted with my people Israel; therefore, the law in me is fulfilled, for I have come to fulfil the law; therefore it hath an end.
(3 Nephi 15:4-5.)

Jesus' Earthly Ministry

Thus we see Jesus was the Firstborn of all spirits
who come to this earth; he sustained the Father's plan
in the council in heaven; he was the Creator and he
was the great Jehovah who manifested himself to the

ancient prophets. Finally, the time came for him to take upon himself a body of flesh and bones and dwell among mortals as had been revealed to the prophets from the beginning of man's sojourn upon earth. As has been discussed in a previous chapter he was born of Mary, grew to manhood, performed his ministry in Palestine, and fulfilled his mission as the Redeemer of man in offering himself as an infinite atonement, having been prepared for this from before the foundation of the world. (See Ether 3:14.)

Jesus' Ministry in the Spirit World

As great as was the Lord's ministry and missionary endeavor in Palestine, it did not come to an end when "he gave up the ghost." Peter tells us:

> For Christ also hath once suffered for sins, the just for the unjust, that he might bring us to God, being put to death in the flesh, but quickened by the Spirit:
> By which also he went and preached unto the spirits in prison;
> Which sometime were disobedient, when once the long-suffering of God waited in the days of Noah, while the ark was a preparing, wherein few, that is, eight souls were saved by water. (1 Peter 3:18-20.)

Furthermore, says Peter: "For this cause was the gospel preached also to them that are dead, that they might be judged according to men in the flesh, but live according to God in the spirit." (*Ibid.*, 4:6.)

On October 3, 1918, President Joseph F. Smith was given a marvelous vision regarding the contents of these very verses. He records:

> As I pondered over these things which are written, the eyes of my understanding were opened, and the Spirit of the Lord rested upon me, and I saw the hosts of the dead, both small and great. And there were gathered together in one place an innumerable company of the spirits of the just, who had been faithful in the testimony of Jesus while they lived in mortality, and who had offered sacrifice in the similitude of the great

sacrifice of the Son of God, and had suffered tribulation in their Redeemer's name. All these had departed the mortal life, firm in the hope of a glorious resurrection, through the grace of God the Father and his Only Begotten Son, Jesus Christ.

* * *

While this vast multitude waited and conversed, rejoicing in the hour of their deliverance from the chains of death, the Son of God appeared declaring liberty to the captives who had been faithful, and there he preached to them the everlasting gospel, the doctrine of the resurrection and the redemption of mankind from the fall, and from individual sins on conditions of repentance. But unto the wicked he did not go, and among the ungodly and the unrepentant who had defiled themselves while in the flesh, his voice was not raised, neither did the rebellious who rejected the testimonies and the warnings of the ancient prophets behold his presence, nor look upon his face.

* * *

And as I wondered, my eyes were opened, and my understanding quickened, and I perceived that the Lord went not in person among the wicked and the disobedient who had rejected the truth, to teach them; but behold, from among the righteous he organized his forces and appointed messengers, clothed with power and authority, and commissioned them to go forth and carry the light of the gospel to them that were in darkness, even to all the spirits of men. And thus was the gospel preached to the dead.

* * *

Thus was it made known that our Redeemer spent his time during his sojourn in the world of spirits, instructing and preparing the faithful spirits of the prophets who had testified of him in the flesh, that they might carry the message of redemption unto all the dead unto whom he could not go personally because of their rebellion and transgression, that they through the ministration of his servants might also hear his words. (*GD*:472-476.)

This marvelous part of Jesus' ministry occurred after his death and prior to his resurrection. After his resurrection, already considered in a previous chapter, he manifested himself to his disciples in Palestine on a number of occasions and on one of those occasions was seen by more than five hundred brethren at once. (See 1 Cor. 15:6. Also see list of his appearances in Talmage's *Jesus the Christ*, p. 699.)

Jesus' Ministry among the Nephites

After his resurrection the Lord also visited the Nephites as had been prophesied among them from the days of Nephi, the son of Lehi. He taught them on three successive days and then returned to visit them on a number of occasions. (3 Nephi 11-28.) Mormon records: "I would that ye should behold that the Lord truly did teach the people, for the space of three days; and after that he did show himself unto them oft, and did break bread oft, and bless it, and give it unto them." (3 Nephi 26:13.)

Jesus and the Lost Tribes of Israel

When Jesus was among the Nephites he told them they were the other sheep of whom he had spoken to his disciples in Palestine. (See John 10:16.) But he also told them that there were still others. He said: "And verily, verily, I say unto you that I have other sheep, which are not of this land, neither of the land of Jerusalem, neither in any parts of that land round about whither I have been to minister." (3 Nephi, 16:1.) Later he said to them: "But now I go unto the Father, and also to show myself unto the lost tribes of Israel, for they are not lost unto the Father, for he knoweth whither he hath taken them." (*Ibid.*, 17:4.)

Jesus and the Last Dispensation

But just as Jesus' work did not end on the cross, nor in the spirit world, it did not end with his visit to the Nephites and the lost tribes of Israel.

The last dispensation, the Dispensation of the Fulness of Times, was ushered in by a visitation of the Father and the Son, Elohim and Jehovah, to the fourteen-year-old Joseph Smith. In part of his account of that event Joseph Smith says: "When the light rested upon me I saw two Personages, whose brightness and glory defy all description, standing above me in the air. One of them spake unto me, calling me by name, and said, pointing to the other—*This is my Beloved Son. Hear Him!*" The Lord then gave the young Joseph some instructions. (Pearl of Great Price, p. 48.)

As already cited above, the Lord also was seen by the Prophet Joseph Smith and Sidney Rigdon when they were given the great vision of the three degrees of glory. (See D&C, Sec. 76.) Still again the Lord manifested himself when he appeared in the Kirtland Temple to Joseph Smith and Oliver Cowdery. The report reads:

The veil was taken from our minds, and the eyes of our understanding were opened.

We saw the Lord standing upon the breastwork of the pulpit, before us; and under his feet was a paved work of pure gold, in color like amber.

His eyes were as a flame of fire; the hair of his head was white like the pure snow; his countenance shone above the brightness of the sun; and his voice was as the sound of the rushing of great waters, even the voice of Jehovah, saying:

I am the first and the last; I am he who liveth, I am he who was slain; I am your advocate with the Father. (*Ibid.*, 110: 1-4.)

Over and over again in the revelations given to the Prophet Joseph Smith the Lord identifies himself. The following are a few examples:

I am Alpha and Omega, Christ the Lord; yea, even I am he, the beginning and the end, the Redeemer of the world. (*Ibid.*, 19:1.)

Listen to the voice of Jesus Christ, your Lord your God, and your Redeemer, whose word is quick and powerful. (*Ibid.*, 27:1.)

Listen to the voice of Jesus Christ, your Redeemer, the Great I Am, whose arm of mercy hath atoned for your sins. (*Ibid.*, 29:1.)

Listen to the voice of the Lord your God, even Alpha and Omega, the beginning and the end, whose course is one eternal round, the same today as yesterday, and forever.

I am Jesus Christ, the Son of God, who was crucified for the sins of the world, even as many as will believe on my name, that they may become the sons of God, even one in me as I am one in the Father, as the Father is one in me, that we may be one. (*Ibid.*, 35:1-2.)

Thus saith the Lord your God, even Jesus Christ, the Great I Am, Alpha and Omega, the beginning and the end, the same which looked upon the wide expanse of eternity, and all the seraphic hosts of heaven, before the world was made;

The same which knoweth all things, for all things are present before mine eyes;

I am the same which spake, and the world was made, and all things came by me. (*Ibid.*, 38:1-3.)

Thus it is evident the Lord actively directed the process of the restoration of his gospel, and as his prophets have continued to testify, he continues to direct the affairs of his kingdom on the earth.

Jesus to Reign on Earth

The prophets have also foreseen and been caused to prophesy that the Lord will usher in the millennium and reign among men upon the earth for a period of a thousand years.

At the time Jesus departed from his disciples in Jerusalem and ascended into heaven two angelic beings appeared and said to the disciples who were looking in amazement: "Ye men of Galilee, why stand ye gazing up into heaven? This same Jesus, which is taken up from you into heaven, shall so come in like manner as ye have seen him go into heaven." (Acts 1:11.)

Peter, preaching to the multitude after healing the lame man at Solomon's porch, rebuking the Jews because they had slain the Redeemer of the world, said unto them: "Repent ye therefore, and be converted, that your sins may be blotted out, when the times of refreshing shall come from the presence of the Lord; And he shall send Jesus Christ, which before was preached unto you: Whom the heaven must receive until the times of restitution of all things, which God hath spoken by the mouth of all his holy prophets since the world began." (Acts 3:19-21.)

John was shown these things and recorded his account in part as follows:

And I saw thrones, and they sat upon them, and judgment was given unto them: and I saw the souls of them that were beheaded for the witness of Jesus, and for the word of God, and which had not worshipped the beast, neither his image, neither had received his mark upon their foreheads, or in their hands; and they lived and reigned with Christ a thousand years.

But the rest of the dead lived not again until the thousand years were finished. This is the first resurrection. (Revelation 20:4-5.)

In our own dispensation the Lord has said this:

For behold, verily, verily, I say unto you, the time is soon at hand that I shall come in a cloud with power and great glory.

And it shall be a great day at the time of my coming, for all nations shall tremble. . . .

And verily, verily, I say unto you, I come quickly. I am your Lord and your Redeemer. Even so. Amen. (D&C 34:7-8, 12.)

Also: "For I will reveal myself from heaven with power and great glory, with all the hosts thereof, and dwell in righteousness with men on earth a thousand years, and the wicked shall not stand." (*Ibid.*, 29:11.)

Too:

For in mine own due time will I come upon the earth in judgment, and my people shall be redeemed and shall reign with me on earth.

For the great Millennium, of which I have spoken by the mouth of my servants, shall come. . . .

Hearken ye to these words. Behold, I am Jesus Christ, the Savior of the world. Treasure these things up in your hearts, and let the solemnities of eternity rest upon your minds. (*Ibid.*, 43:29-30; 34.)

These will be great events, and they have been seen and hopefully looked to at least from the days of Enoch, who, when he was shown what was to happen to the Beloved Son when he would come into the world, wept and cried unto the Lord asking, "When shall the earth rest?" Later in the great vision the Lord declared to Enoch "for the space of a thousand years the earth shall rest. And it came to pass that Enoch saw the day of the coming of the Son of Man, in the last days, to dwell on the earth in righteousness for the space of a thousand years." (Moses 7:64-65.)

Jesus Is the Judge

Even having reigned on earth for a thousand years, the work of the Lord Jesus Christ will not be entirely finished. For, as John the Revelator says: "When the thousand years are expired, Satan shall be loosed out of his prison, And shall go out to deceive the nations which are in the four quarters of the earth, Gog and Magog, to gather them together to battle: the number of whom is as the sand of the sea." (Revelation 20:7-8; see vss, 9-10 also.) After a "little season" of the devil's rampaging he will be cast out forever.

The Lord at that time will perform another great function of his Godhood when he judges the world. On one occasion he declared: "For the Father judgeth no man, but hath committed all judgment unto the Son. . . . Verily, verily, I say unto you, The hour is coming, and now is, when the dead shall hear the voice of the Son of God: and they that hear shall live. For as the Father hath life in himself; so hath he given to the Son to have life in himself; And hath given him authority to execute judgment also, because he is the Son of man . . . . I can of mine own self do nothing: as I hear, I judge:

and my judgment is just; because I seek not mine own will, but the will of the Father which hath sent me." (John 5:22, 25-27, 30.)

Peter, in preaching to Cornelius and others, said, speaking of Jesus: "And he commanded us to preach unto the people, and to testify that it is he which was ordained of God to be the Judge of quick and dead." (Acts 10:42.)

King Benjamin, speaking of the Lord, declared to his people:

> And moreover, I say unto you, that there shall be no other name given nor any other way nor means whereby salvation can come unto the children of men, only in and through the name of Christ, the Lord Omnipotent. For behold he judgeth, and his judgment is just. . . . (Mosiah 3:17-18.)

Mormon, lamenting over the destruction of his people, records:

> And the day soon cometh that your mortal must put on immortality, and these bodies which are now moldering in corruption must soon become incorruptible bodies; and then ye must stand before the judgment-seat of Christ, to be judged according to your works; and if it so be that ye are righteous, then are ye blessed with your fathers who have gone before you. (Mormon 6:21.)

Moroni, in concluding his book refers to the Lord as "the great Jehovah, the Eternal Judge of both quick and dead." (Moroni 10:34.)

Conclusion

Thus we see that from the very beginning of man's pre-mortal existence the Firstborn, Jesus Christ, Jehovah, has directed the work for the saving of his Father's children. In summary:

1. In the great council in the pre-mortal world he defended his Father's will in opposition to Lucifer in the interest of his Father's spirit children.

2. He created or organized the worlds.

3. He was the great Jehovah who gave revelation to all the prophets prior to his birth as the Son of Mary.

4. He was the promised Messiah and suffered the atonement to redeem mankind from death and sin.

5. He visited the spirit world and organized that kingdom for the preaching of his gospel.

6. He visited the Nephites and personally taught the gospel to them.

7. He visited the lost tribes of Israel.

8. He restored the gospel to the Prophet Joseph Smith and has continued to reveal his will to the prophets.

9. He will usher in the millennium and reign on the earth for a thousand years.

10. At the end of the world when all men are resurrected through his power, he will judge all men according to their works.

We sometimes think of the mortal span as a long time to endure to the end, but compare this with Jesus' work.

Chapter V

THE HOLY GHOST AND BEING BORN
OF THE SPIRIT

Associated with Elohim (Heavenly Father) and Jehovah (Jesus Christ) in the Godhead is a Personage known to mortals as the Holy Ghost. Sometimes he is called by other names such as Holy Spirit, or the Spirit, etc., but it is better to call him the Holy Ghost and use the other names to refer to the influence which comes from the heavenly Presence.

In this chapter we will be concerned with such questions as: How is the Holy Ghost distinguished from the Father and the Son? In what special way does the Holy Ghost contribute to the salvation and exaltation of man? What is the nature of man? Why must one be born again? What does it mean to be born again? What are the blessings which are available to those who have the gift of the Holy Ghost?

In some "Important Items of Instruction" given by the Prophet Joseph Smith the Holy Ghost is distinguished from the Father and the Son as follows:

The Father has a body of flesh and bones as tangible as man's; the Son also; but the Holy Ghost has not a body of flesh and bones, but is a personage of Spirit. Were it not so, the Holy Ghost could not dwell in us. (D&C 130:22.)

There are many gifts and blessings which come to man through the Holy Ghost (1 Cor. 12; Mark 16:16-18; Mormon 9:24-29; D&C 46:11-33), but there is one way particularly in which the Holy Ghost contributes to the salvation and exaltation of man. He assists man in that priceless process of being born again.

In the Lord's well-known counsel to Nicodemus, he said: "Except a man be born of water and of

the Spirit, he cannot enter into the kingdom of God.
That which is born of the flesh is flesh; and that which
is born of the Spirit is spirit." (John 3:5-6.)

Regarding the Nature of Man

But according to the word of the Lord and his
prophets, what is the nature of man? In a modern revelation the Lord said:

> Every spirit of man was innocent in the beginning; and
> God having redeemed man from the fall, men became again, in
> their infant state, innocent before God.
> And that wicked one cometh and taketh away light and
> truth, through disobedience, from the children of men, and be-
> cause of the tradition of their fathers. (D&C 93:38-39.)

Thus, from the beginning of man's mortal existence the wicked one, the devil, has engaged in taking
away "light and truth." He has done this through men,
individually and collectively—individually through disobedience and collectively through the tradition of their
fathers.

Fundamentally, the revelation teaches us that infants are innocent, but that they are born in a mortal
world where men are agents unto themselves, even acknowledging various influences which may contribute
to decision-making, and where, through the exercise of
agency, men individually have chosen in varying degrees to acknowledge or deny God, and similarly have
chosen to accept and practice or reject his principles in
varying degrees. Consequently, although babes are innocent, by the time they reach the age of accountability
they have become acquainted, through personal weaknesses and those of others, with a fallen world. Although not comprehending these words, they no doubt
quite adequately understand that man has his failings.
Perhaps this is in part what King Benjamin had in
mind when he said:

For the natural man is an enemy to God, and has been from the fall of Adam, and will be, forever and ever, unless he yields to the enticings of the Holy Spirit, and putteth off the natural man and becometh a saint through the atonement of Christ the Lord, and becometh as a child, submissive, meek, humble, patient, full of love, willing to submit to all things which the Lord seeth fit to inflict upon him, even as a child doth submit to his father. (Mosiah 3:19.)

Another passage speaks of the natural man as carnal, sensual, and devilish. These words may seem harsh, but it is probably impossible for us even to guess what the corrupt state of man would be had there not been periodic restorations of the gospel in man's history and some glimmer of spiritual knowledge trickling down through the centuries.

It is important that the teaching of Mosiah be distinguished from the apostate doctrine of depravity. Man is not born evil, but innocent. He is innocent until he reaches the age of accountability, but he grows up in a world of sin and as an agent makes choices from among a vast complex of enticements, and when he becomes accountable and refuses to make his will submissive to God by accepting him and making covenants with him, he is carnal, sensual, and devilish.

An examination of the matter suggests, however, that the words "carnal," "sensual," and "devilish," must not be limited to their more narrow and specific connotations, but that they are accurately, though more broadly, interpreted by the scriptural phrase "enemy to God." That is, not all men who have not made the covenants with the Christ are given to indulging in practices which are appropriately designated carnal, sensual, and devilish. Yet, all men, regardless of how moral and how pure they may be with reference to those practices called carnal, sensual, and devilish, are enemies to God until they yield to the enticings of the Holy Spirit, accept the atonement of the Lord, and are submissive to his will. A significant point here is, what we conventionally call basic personal and social morality is not enough. In addition to these things one must do other things which are binding upon him by virtue of his covenantal relationship with the Father and the Son. Or, putting it otherwise, for one not to be an enemy to God he must do all things whatsoever the Lord his God shall command him. (See Abraham 3:25.)

Summarily put, the natural man (he who is carnal, sensual, and devilish; he who is an enemy to God) is the man who has not humbled himself before God and made covenants with God by receiving the revealed ordinances at the hands of God's authorized servants, and if, having done this, has failed to conduct himself in such a way as to heed the counsel or command given when he was confirmed a member of the Church to "Receive the Holy Ghost."

One Must Be Born Again

One must put off the natural man. He may be born of the water by baptism in the water by one who holds the Holy Priesthood and may also receive the *ordinance* of the laying on of hands for the gift of the Holy Ghost by an authorized servant of the Lord, but the Priesthood bearer cannot give him the Holy Ghost, only the right to receive that gift. The Holy Ghost will be manifest in his life only as he strives for that gift and will come to him through the Holy Ghost himself. Therefore, one's being born of the Spirit comes only from the Spirit.

Adam was instructed to teach this principle of rebirth to his posterity, as Moses informs us in the remarkable passage:

... by reason of transgression cometh the fall, which fall bringeth death, and inasmuch as ye were born into the world by water, and blood, and the spirit, which I have made, and so became of dust a living soul, even so ye must be born again into the kingdom of heaven, of water, and of Spirit, and be cleansed by blood, even the blood of mine Only Begotten; that ye might be sanctified from all sin, and enjoy the words of eternal life in this world, and eternal life in the world to come, even immortal glory;

For by the water ye keep the commandment; by the Spirit ye are justified, and by the blood ye are sanctified. (Moses 6:59-60.)

This wonderful passage forcefully indicates that it is essential for men to be born again, and that this consists of the water, the Spirit, and the blood, and that by the water the mortal keeps the commandment, and by the Spirit (Holy Ghost) he is justified, and that by the blood (the atonement of the Christ) he is sanctified.

What It Means to Be Born Again

That the spiritual rebirth involves more than the mere acceptance of an ordinance (laying on of hands) and requires a change in the man is evident from the words of Alma. In one place he says (note that he was addressing his remarks to the "brethren of the church"): "And now behold, I ask of you, my brethren of the church, have ye spiritually been born of God? Have ye received his image in your countenances? Have ye experienced this mighty change in your hearts?"

Speaking of the judgment when men will have been raised from their graves, he adds: "I say unto you, can ye look up to God at that day with a pure heart and clean hands? I say unto you, can you look up, having the image of God engraven upon your countenances?" (Alma 5:14, 19.)

The necessity of this change is stated emphatically by Alma as follows:

And the Lord said unto me: Marvel not that all mankind, yea, men and women, all nations, kindreds, tongues and people, must be born again; yea, born of God, changed from their carnal and fallen state, to a state of righteousness, being redeemed of God, becoming his sons and daughters;

And thus they become new creatures; and unless they do this, they can in nowise inherit the kingdom of God. (Mosiah 27: 25-26.)

Alma's language seems to be plain enough that his meaning cannot be mistaken. He is speaking of a real change in which men become "new creatures."

In another passage, again addressing himself to the members of the Church, he says:

And now I say unto you that this is the order after which I am called, yea, to preach unto my beloved brethren, yea, and every one that dwelleth in the land; yea, to preach unto all, both old and young, both bond and free; yea, I say unto you the aged, and also the middle aged, and the rising generation; yea, to cry unto them that they must repent and be born again. (Alma 5:49.)

This suggests that there were members of the Church who were aged, and middle-aged, as well as those of the rising generation who still had not been born of the Spirit.

One may receive the ordinance of the laying on of hands for the gift of the Holy Ghost, but the responsibility clearly rests upon him to live in such a way that he will receive the blessings of the Holy Ghost in his life; for example, President Joseph F. Smith said: "The presentation or 'gift' of the Holy Ghost simply confers upon a man the right to receive at any time, when he is worthy of it and desires it, the power and light of truth of the Holy Ghost, although he may often be left to his own spirit and judgment." (*GD*: 60-61.) He also said: "It will depend upon the worthiness of him unto whom the gift is bestowed whether he receive the Holy Ghost or not." (*GD*: 61.)

One Needs the Blessings of the Spirit

From the beginning of the restoration the Saints have been urged to live so that they might enjoy the blessings of the Spirit. President Wilford Woodruff related some interesting experiences in this regard. He said:

One morning, while we were at Winter Quarters, Brother Brigham Young said to me and the brethren that he had had a visitation the night previous from Joseph Smith. I asked him what he said to him. He replied that Joseph had told him to tell the people to labor to obtain the Spirit of God; that they needed that to sustain them and to give them power to go through their work in the earth.

Now I will give you a little of my experience in this line. Joseph Smith visited me a great deal after his death, and taught me many important principles . . . Joseph and Hyrum visited me, and the Prophet laid before me a great many things. Among other things he told me to get the Spirit of God; that all of us needed it. . . .

* * *

Brigham Young also visited me after his death. On one occasion he and Brother Heber C. Kimball came in a splendid chariot, with fine white horses, and accompanied me to a conference that I was going to attend. When I got there I asked Brother Brigham if he would take charge of the conference. "No," said he, "I have done my work here. I have come to see what you are doing and what you are teaching the people." And he told me what Joseph Smith had taught him in Winter Quarters, to teach the people to get the Spirit of God. He said, "I want you to teach the people to get the Spirit of God. You cannot build up the Kingdom of God without that."

That is what I want to say to the brethren and sisters here today. Every man and woman in this Church should labor to get that Spirit. (Weber Stake Conference address, reported in the *Deseret Weekly News*, Vol. 53, No. 21, Nov. 7, 1896.)

Men and women may repent of their sins and signify this to the world by making covenants with the Lord through baptism and confirmation by God's authorized servants, but they must be steadfast in righteousness. They must, paraphrasing King Benjamin, retain a remission of their sins from day to day that they may walk guiltless before God. (Mosiah 4:26.)

President David O. McKay, speaking of this, said:

. . . He [the Lord] told Nicodemus that before he could solve the question that was troubling his mind, his spiritual vision would have to be *changed by an entire revolution of his "inner man."* His manner of thinking, feeling, and acting with reference to spiritual things would have to undergo *a fundamental and permanent change* with reference to spiritual matters.

It is easy to see temporal things. It is easy to yield to lascivious things. It requires little or no effort to indulge in anything physical and animal-like. But to be born out of that world into a spiritual world is advancement that the Lord *requires* of each of us. (*CR,* April, 1960, p. 26. Italics added.)

Elder Marion G. Romney speaks of the continual conflict in which mortals are involved and indicates what is necessary for them to maintain a condition of righteousness in their lives. He says:

The great over-all struggle in the world today is as it has always been, for the souls of men. Every soul is personally engaged in the struggle, and he makes the fight with what is in his mind. In the final analysis the battleground is, for each individual, within himself. Inevitably he gravitates towards the subjects of his thoughts. Ages ago the wise man thus succinctly put this great truth: "For as he thinketh in his heart, so is he." (Prov. 23:7.)

If we would escape the lusts of the flesh and build for ourselves and for our children great and noble characters, we must keep in our minds and in their minds true and righteous principles for our thoughts and their thoughts to dwell upon.

*   *   *

If we would avoid adopting the evils of the world, we must pursue a course which will daily feed our minds with and call them back to the things of the spirit. I know of no better way to do this than by reading the Book of Mormon.

*   *   *

And so, I counsel you, my beloved brothers and sisters and friends everywhere, to make reading in the Book of Mormon a few minutes each day a lifelong practice. All of us need continuing close contact with the Spirit of the Lord. We need to take the Holy Spirit for our guide that we be not deceived. (*CR,* April, 1960, pp. 111, 112.)

Those who receive the initiatory ordinances of baptism and the laying on of hands for the gift of the Holy Ghost are formally eligible to receive great blessings, for as President Wilford Woodruff said:

The Holy Ghost . . . is different from the common Spirit of God, which we are told lighteth every man that cometh into the world. *The Holy Ghost is only given to men through their obedience to the Gospel of Christ;* and every man who received that Spirit has a comforter within—a leader to dictate and guide him. This Spirit reveals, day by day, to every man who has faith, those things which are for his benefit. As Job said, "There is a spirit in man and the inspiration of the Almighty giveth it understanding." It is this inspiration of God to His children in every age of the world that is one of the necessary gifts to sustain man and enable him to walk by faith and to go forth and obey all the dictations and commandments and revelations which God gives to His children to guide and direct them in life. (*JD* 13:157, December 12, 1869. Italics ours.)

The role and power of the Holy Ghost in the lives of men and women who have received not only the right to the gift but also the gift of the Holy Ghost itself is succinctly put by the Prophet Joseph Smith in the following words: "No man can receive the Holy Ghost without receiving revelations. The Holy Ghost is a revelator." (*DHC* VI:58.)

To assist men and women in retaining the remission of sins from day to day there are many individual gifts which may come to one through the gift of the Holy Ghost. Prefacing a discussion of and an enumeration of some of those gifts in a modern revelation the Lord says:

But ye are commanded in all things to ask of God, who giveth liberally; and that which the Spirit testifies unto you even so I would that ye should do in all holiness of heart, walking uprightly before me, considering the end of your salvation, doing all things with prayer and thanksgiving, that ye may not be

seduced by evil spirits, or doctrines of devils, or the commandments of men; for some are of men, and others of devils.

Wherefore, beware lest ye are deceived; and that ye may
not be deceived seek ye earnestly the best gifts, always remem-
bering for what they are given;

For verily I say unto you, they are given for the benefit
of those who love me and keep all my commandments, and him
that seeketh so to do; that all may be benefited that seek or
that ask of me, that ask and not for a sign that they may con-
sume it upon their lusts. (D&C 46:7-9.)

Conclusion

The gift of the Holy Ghost is another marvelous
witness of the Lord's great love for mankind. From time
to time since the days of Adam the Lord has raised up
prophets to whom he has revealed his will and through
whom his gospel has been taught. The Lord himself
came to the earth and lived among mortals and gave
his life in the infinite atonement that men *would* be
resurrected and that they *could* be forgiven for their
sins. He has provided the means for men to make covenants with him by which they may obtain a remission
of their sins, be permitted to take his name upon themselves, and be initiated into his earthly kingdom. And
finally, those who receive the initiatory ordinances of
baptism and the laying on of hands for the gift of the
Holy Ghost and strive to the utmost to live faithful to
those covenants have the gifts of the Holy Ghost granted
unto them to bless them in this world and assist them
to resist the powers of the adversary and endure to the
end, that ultimately they *will be* heirs to God's heavenly
kingdom.

PART II MAN

Chapter VI

"HOW DOES A MAN GET TO KNOW GOD?"

Immediately upon reading this title some persons will probably exclaim, "How presumptuous!" Even a cursory analysis of the title will reveal that it assumes two basic propositions: first, God is; and second, man can know him. However, it is not the purpose of this brief chapter to examine these propositions.

Whether a given person considers the title presumptuous or not there are many individuals who, in varying degrees, accept the two propositions assumed in the title and with corresponding degrees of eagerness desire to know God. Furthermore, the Lord Jesus Christ suggested man could know him and the Father when he said:

And this is life eternal, that they might know thee the only true God, and Jesus Christ, whom thou hast sent. (John 17:3.)

To one who has studied the written revelations I believe the title is full of meaning, for in God's mercy he has revealed many things to encourage his children to seek him and has manifested the ways they might come to know him.

The following six steps are fundamental in man's getting to know God.

1. Believe that God exists.
2. Believe that he is the *kind of being* man can come to know.
3. Believe man *can* come to know him.
4. Acknowledge him.
5. Desire to know him.
6. Strive to know him.

That one must believe that God exists to entertain the question, "How Does a Man Get to Know God?" is obvious, but it is the logical beginning of the answer to the question and needs to be stated.

Less obvious but equally necessary, it must be recognized that if God is to be known he must be a kind of being that *can* be known. In other words, he must not be a conceptual abstraction only, but must have substantive reality.

Furthermore, one must not only believe that God is the kind of being that can be known, but he must believe that it is possible for man to come to know him.

Believing that God is, that he is the kind of being that can be known, and that man can know him, one must acknowledge him by offering his prayers of thanksgiving to him.

One who becomes aware of God's existence and acknowledges him devotedly is usually motivated to want to know him. He begins to realize his own inadequacies as well as God's greatness and desires within his soul to draw near unto God and know the power and sweetness of his presence.

Much could be said regarding each of the foregoing necessary steps, but inasmuch as they are preliminary to the crux of the answer to our question the remainder of our brief treatment must be devoted to it.

One who has achieved an earnest and honest desire to know God is ready to *strive* to know him. What are some of the minimal things of which his striving must consist?

As one strives to find God, he should study the works of others who claim to have found him, that is, the prophets. The words of the Lord as given to us by the prophets declare that we must have faith in Jesus Christ. This is not simply faith in God, but faith in Jesus as the Christ. There are many scriptures illustrative of this point but Jesus' words as recorded by John are as fitting and clear as any, where he said:

> ... if ye believe not that I am he, ye shall die in your sins. (John 8:24. See also Acts 4:10-12; Romans 6:23.)

But as one begins to develop faith in Jesus he must come to a realization of his own shortcomings and sins and his need to repent. He must vigorously exert himself to correct his wrongs and improve himself.

To be complete the initial process of repentance must culminate in the person's being baptized, for the Lord said:

> He that believeth and is baptized shall be saved; but he that believeth not shall be damned.   (Mark 16:16.)

But the Lord said two baptisms are essential if one is to enter the kingdom of God, not only a baptism by water, but also a baptism of the Spirit. (See John 3: 1-13.) The baptism of the Spirit, or the right to receive the gift of the Holy Ghost, is conferred upon a person by the laying on of hands by one bearing the Melchizedek Priesthood.

Although one may be given a testimony that the gospel is true prior to being baptized, these principles and ordinances are essential if one is to enjoy the *gift* of the Holy Ghost, to say nothing of that great gift of coming to know God, for in this day, speaking of the priesthood and the ordinances of the gospel, the Lord has declared:

> ... [The Melchizedek] priesthood administereth the gospel and holdeth the key of the mysteries of the kingdom, even the key of the knowledge of God.
>
> Therefore, in the ordinances thereof, the power of godliness is manifest.
>
> And without the ordinances thereof, and the authority of the priesthood, the power of godliness is not manifest unto men in the flesh;

For without this no man can see the face of God, even the Father, and live. (D&C 84:19-22.)

Therefore, one must have faith in the Lord, repent of his sins, and receive the ordinances administered by God's holy priesthood. These things are necessary, but to come to know God and enjoy the companionship of his Spirit he must retain a remission of sins from day to day by striving to observe all things which the Lord has commanded and counseled.

If one really desires to know God let him always remember that the Lord has said:

Behold, I stand at the door, and knock: if any man hear my voice, and open the door, I will come in to him, and will sup with him, and he with me. (Revelation 3:20.)

And:

He that hath my commandments, and keepeth them, he it is that loveth me: and he that loveth me shall be loved of my Father, and I will love him, and will manifest myself to him. (John 14:21. See also I John 3:2-3; D&C 38:7-8; 67:11-12; 76:94-96; 88:67-68; 93:1.)

Chapter VII

THE TWO GREAT COMMANDMENTS

Jesus said, "If ye love me, keep my commandments." (John 14:15.) What does that sentence mean? —not just what does it mean in the abstract—what does it mean to you concretely?

For thousands of years the world has had the benefit of a great revelation God gave to Moses. It is known as the Decalogue or, more popularly, as the Ten Commandments. It is found in the twentieth chapter of Exodus in the Old Testament. Those commandments are:

1. "Thou shalt have no other gods before me."
2. "Thou shalt not make unto thee any graven image. . . ."
3. "Thou shalt not take the name of the Lord thy God in vain. . . ."
4. "Remember the sabbath day, to keep it holy."
5. "Honour thy father and thy mother. . . ."
6. "Thou shalt not kill."
7. "Thou shalt not commit adultery."
8. "Thou shalt not steal."
9. "Thou shalt not bear false witness. . . ."
10. "Thou shalt not covet. . . ." (See Exodus 20.)

It is interesting to observe the order of the commandments, for a definite pattern is discernable. The first four commandments deal with one's relation to God and the worship of God; the last six deal with one's relation to his fellow men. It should be noted that the fifth commandment, the first of those regarding one's relation to his fellow men, concerns one's relation to his parents.

This observation is consistent with what Jesus taught when he was approached by a lawyer and asked, "Master, which is the great commandment in the law?" (Matthew 22:36.)

Jesus said unto him, Thou shalt love the Lord thy God with all thy heart, and with all thy soul, and with all thy mind.

This is the first and great commandment.

And the second is like unto it, Thou shalt love thy neighbour as thyself.

On these two commandments hang all the law and the prophets. (*Ibid.*, 22:37-40.)

Therefore, all the commandments of the Decalogue, and all the *other* commandments of God hang upon those two commandments.

What are some of the other commandments?

Men are taught to be meek, merciful, peacemaking, pure in heart, to suffer persecution for the sake of righteousness, to cast those things out of their lives which are offensive, not to swear, and to love their enemies. Also, the Lord said: do good to them that hate you, pray for them which despitefully use you and persecute you, be perfect, do almsgiving privately, pray sincerely avoiding show and vain repetitions, forgive your fellow men, fast without show, seek righteousness first, judge not, give not that which is holy to the dogs, ask, seek, and knock. All of these things and more the Lord advocated in his Sermon on the Mount. (*Ibid.*, 5, 6, 7.)

In modern times God has revealed to man that he should abstain from taking certain substances into his body indicating that they are harmful. This revelation is known as the Word of Wisdom. (See D&C, Section 89.)

Also, in this dispensation the Lord has reaffirmed his commandment that men should observe his law of tithing, giving one tenth of their annual increase (income) for the building up of God's kingdom on the earth. (See *ibid.*, Section 119.)

There are many commandments God has given to mankind, either through his Son or through the prophets, yet all of them hang upon what Jesus called the first two commandments.

Some people may suggest that there is no need for them to belong to any church nor declare belief in any form of religion to do the things mentioned here. And, when it comes to the majority of the things listed here they are exactly right. As a matter of fact, there are good people the world over, of many religious professions, who claim belief in and achieve varying measures of success in striving to observe these principles. But their striving and achievement can be thought of only in terms of the second commandment, loving one's neighbor as himself.

But, someone will say, how can you say that? Are not the first two commandments the same? Is not one necessarily keeping the first commandment when he keeps the second?

The two commandments are not the same. If there was no difference between them, there would have been no need for the Lord to distinguish them as two commandments.

Furthermore, one who keeps the second commandment necessarily keeps the first *only in a limited way.* This answer is required for at least two reasons: (1) The first commandment is more inclusive than the second, for if one loves the Lord with all of his heart, soul, and mind he will do *all* things which God has commanded. The first commandment therefore includes some things which are required of man *in addition to* those involving one's relation to his fellow men. (2) There are people in the world who observe the second commandment on other than religious grounds, who totally ignore those things which are specifically part of the first commandment.

If one can keep most of the commandments, those basically oriented in mercy and justice, and live the

kind of life which would be called exemplary—the good
life—without the Church and other commandments,
what is the basic role of the Church?

Essentially, the answer to that question is something like this: the gospel of Jesus Christ involves and
requires much more of a man than what is customarily
called the good life.

As already indicated, the good life (the second
commandment, speaking generally) *is necessary*, but
if one is to please God and achieve his own highest purposes he must keep the first commandment also.

Now, what is specifically required in the first commandment which is not a necessary part of the second
commandment? Here are a few fundamental things:

1. Faith in the Lord Jesus Christ. This is not
merely faith—but it is faith in Jesus as the Christ, the
Redeemer, the Son of God, who suffered for the sins of
all the world and broke the bands of death in his resurrection.

2. Repentance. This is a principle which involves
forsaking wrongdoing, and also requires the *doing* of
those things which are proper, right, and good. This is
a glorious principle and is applicable to every facet of
mortal life. But again, as important as this is as it relates to human conduct, that is not its full meaning. For
although one may be motivated for one reason or another to change his conduct for the better, even after he
has made all restitutions which are possible for his
former offenses, his repentance is still incomplete.

The Lord has been very explicit about this. He
said: "for if ye believe not that I am he, ye shall die in
your sins." (John 8:24.) So regardless of what else
one does in an effort to improve himself and obtain a
forgiveness of sins he must turn unto the Christ. The
Lord stresses this point over and over again, that there
is only one way to his Father and that is through him,

Jesus. Forgiveness of sins comes only through Jesus Christ, so in order to obtain that forgiveness and have one's repentance complete he must turn unto the Lord.

If having faith in the redeeming power of Jesus Christ, and turning from wrongdoing with all one's soul is not turning to the Lord, what is lacking?

3. Baptism. Remember, the Lord said, if ye love me keep my commandments, and to be baptized is one of the commandments. He taught that baptism was necessary to salvation. Mark speaks of it as "baptism of repentance for the remission of sins." (Mark 1:4.) And the Lord declared: "He that believeth and is baptized shall be saved, but he that believeth not shall be damned." (*Ibid.*, 16:16.)

In a modern revelation, speaking regarding the same subject, Jesus said: "And by this you may know they are under the bondage of sin, because they come not unto me. For whoso cometh not unto me is under the bondage of sin." (D&C 84:50-51.)

Baptism is the gate; it is the outward expression or sign of the covenant one makes with Jesus; it is the completion of repentance. For one to say he has faith in Jesus as the Redeemer, and that he desires to repent and be forgiven of his sins means that he wants to be baptized. So, if he means what he says, he will be baptized at the hands of one who holds the priesthood of God which has been restored in this dispensation.

But he who has been baptized by a properly authorized servant of God is eligible to receive another gift:

4. The laying on of hands for the gift of the Holy Ghost. This is a choice blessing of inestimable value. Among other things, the bearer of the Melchizedek Priesthood who performs this ordinance says to the newly baptized person, "Receive the Holy Ghost." In effect, this is a command to the person to receive the Holy Ghost or Comforter and give him the right to en-

joy the companionship and guidance of the Comforter as he lives for it and have the benefit of the gifts of the Spirit.

The Lord said to a leader of the ancient Jews:

Verily, verily, I say unto thee, Except a man be born of water and of the Spirit, he cannot enter into the kingdom of God. (John 3:5.)

Therefore, if one is not to be damned (see Mark 16:16 above) and is to enter the kingdom of God, he must do more than keep those commandments which are summarized in the charge to love one's neighbor as himself.

He must have faith in Jesus as the Redeemer; he must repent of his sins; he must be baptized by an authorized servant of God, and receive the laying on of hands for the gift of the Holy Ghost by one holding the Melchizedek Priesthood.

Remember Jesus said:

He that loveth father or mother more than me is not worthy of me: and he that loveth son or daughter more than me is not worthy of me.

And he that taketh not his cross, and followeth after me, is not worthy of me. (Matthew 10:37-38.)

The Lord has given mankind many commandments and they are for the benefit of man. He even gave his life on the cross that man could be redeemed through him.

When one begins to grasp his own inadequacies and the majesty and love of the Lord, he longs not merely to keep the second commandment by imitating good works, but he longs for the rebirth—to be born of the spirit—changed in the inner man. This can only come in time as one keeps the first and great commandment, and meets those requirements the Lord has set, which demonstrate that he loves the Lord with all of his heart, soul, and mind.

Chapter VIII

PRAYER

Many people consider prayer a period of quiet reflection, introspection, and contemplation. They regard
it as a means of lifting themselves by their own boot-
straps. That is, by taking the time to pause and ponder,
individuals become aware of certain of their propensi-
ties or inclinations and through such self-awareness
become better prepared to overcome their weaknesses
or put them in their proper places. No doubt there
is merit in such activity. People should pause occasion-
ally and attempt to evaluate themselves, determine their
strengths and weaknesses, set goals of improvement
to be achieved, and plan systematic ways to reach those
ends. But can such reflection, even with a bowed head
or kneeling body, properly be called prayer?

Prayer is more than contemplation to the Latter-
day Saint. It is communion with the Divine; it is communion with God. In fact, it is more than communion.
It is communication—communication between man and
God, and one avenue of communication between God and
man. The word "communion" connotes community or
harmony of attitude or spirit with the Divine, or perhaps may describe one's feeling, but the word "communication" means more than that. In addition to the
above, "communication" means interchange of thoughts
or ideas, which, simply put, means that man expresses
his thoughts to God and not infrequently experiences,
feels, or has impressed upon him, thoughts or inspiration from God.

Prayer is real. It is powerful. It bears fruit in
direct proportion to the seriousness with which it is considered, and likewise with the faith, diligence, and
obedience of the one who prays. Man does not merely

commune with a world spirit, or an imaginary being without body, parts, or passions, but he communicates with a real Being, one who is in form like man, with a glorified body of flesh and bones, and one who is capable of not mere communion, but communication. He is God the Eternal Father; the Father of the spirits of all mankind.

As we go through our daily routines, doing the things which are required of us to maintain our livelihood, and performing those other tasks which we have assumed, school, church, and other responsibilities, we are continually met with problems. This life we are living is called by the Book of Mormon prophets a probationary state, that is, a period when men are on trial, so to speak. It is a period when men are given an opportunity to meet situations which require making decisions, and on the basis of those decisions, depending upon what they are, men either progress or retrogress, they develop or hinder their development. So, it is in the nature of things for men to be faced with problems and difficulties. The significant thing is not the fact that we have problems, but the question, how do we face them? What is our attitude when we have to meet them? Do we have a calm assurance that in some way the situation will be satisfactorily met, or do we become so unnerved and inwardly disturbed that we cannot employ all of our resources to the best advantage? Surely all people would prefer to have the confidence and assurance that things will be worked out satisfactorily.

One modern writer has illustrated this point very well in the following excerpt:

Once, as a young man full of exuberant fancy, I undertook to draw up a catalogue of the acknowledged "goods" of life. As other men sometimes tabulate lists of properties they own or would like to own, I set down my inventory of earthly desirables: health, love, beauty, talent, power, riches, and fame—together with several minor ingredients of what I considered man's perfect portion.

When my inventory was completed I proudly showed it to a wise elder who had been the mentor and spiritual model of my youth. Perhaps I was trying to impress him with my precocious wisdom and the large universality of my interests. Anyway, I handed him the list. "This," I told him confidently, "is the sum of mortal goods. Could a man possess them all, he would be as a god."

At the corners of my friend's old eyes, I saw wrinkles of amusement gathering in a patient net. "An excellent list," he said, pondering it thoughtfully. "Well digested in content and set down in a not-unreasonable order. But it appears, my young friend, that you have omitted the most important element of all. You have forgotten the one ingredient lacking which each possession becomes a hideous torment, and your list as a whole an intolerable burden."

"And what," I asked, peppering my voice with truculence, "is that missing ingredient?"

With a pencil stub he crossed out my entire schedule. Then, having demolished my adolescent dream structure at a single stroke, he wrote down three syllables: *peace of mind.*

"This is the gift that God reserves for His special proteges," he said. "Talent and beauty He gives to many. Wealth is commonplace, fame not rare. But peace of mind—that is His final guerdon of approval, the fondest sign of His love. He bestows it charily. Most men are never blessed with it; others wait all their lives—yes, far into advanced age—for this gift to descend upon them."

*   *   *

At that time I found it difficult wholly to believe the wisdom of my rabbinic friend. But a quarter of a century of personal experience and professional observation has served only to confirm his almost oracular utterance. I have come to understand that peace of mind is the characteristic mark of God Himself. . . . I know now that the sum of all other possessions does not necessarily add up to peace of mind; yet, on the other hand, I have seen this inner tranquility flourish without the material supports of property or even the buttress of physical health. Slowly, painfully, I have learned that peace of mind may transform a cottage into a spacious manor hall; the want of it can make a regal park an imprisoning nutshell. (Joshua

Loth Liebman, *Peace of Mind* [New York: Simon and Schuster, Inc., 1946] pp. 3-5.)

This was written by a man near the end of his life, a life full of experience in counseling people. It is a clearly and beautifully phrased illustration that an inner feeling of security, or a calm assurance, or peace of mind, is one of the supreme gifts that mortals can enjoy.

Latter-day Saints believe that prayer is a necessary prerequisite to peace of mind. Prayer is the means whereby a man draws himself close to God. He unfolds the secrets of his heart to Heavenly Father, confiding in him. Prayer is man's way of seeking the partnership of Heavenly Father in all of his undertakings. When a man so prays and works diligently to accomplish all things in accordance with Heavenly Father's will, he cannot but be blessed with the serenity of mind which he desires.

This calm assurance or peace of mind is what might be called an over-all gift, one which affects man in a general way and permeates all that he does. It helps him do everything that he does better than he would do those things otherwise. We can see from all that has been said that this is a blessing or benefit one derives from prayer which cannot be measured.

In addition to this wonderful blessing which men can enjoy through prayer, accompanied by obedience and diligence, there is a host of blessings or benefits or fruits of prayer which men can and do enjoy. There is perhaps a number of ways in which these fruits of prayer might be classified, but for our purposes let us consider them in two categories. The first category we shall designate the Personal Blessings. The second category we shall designate the Social Blessings. Certainly these names are arbitrarily given, for all blessings are personal and all blessings have social implications, even if they are not directly social. But these names, Personal and Social, will serve as guides, and under each we shall discuss those blessings we consider more directly personal or social.

I. *Personal Blessings*

(1) Protection against the adversary.

In the Sermon on the Mount when the Lord Jesus Christ taught his disciples how to pray, among other things he said, "And lead us not into temptation, but deliver us from evil." (Matthew 6:13.) Implicit in this admonition is the promise that if men will so pray they will not be led into temptation but will be led away from evil paths.

When the Lord went to the Garden of Gethsemane to pray to his Father, he took Peter, James, and John with him to be watchers for him. When he came to them and found them asleep he counseled, "Watch and pray, that ye enter not into temptation: the spirit indeed is willing, but the flesh is weak." (*Ibid.*, 26:41.)

Not once, but many times in modern revelation the Lord has counseled his servants similarly.

One verse of modern scripture shows with unmistakable clearness that prayer is a means of fortifying ourselves against the adversary. This advice given to the Prophet Joseph Smith will surely hold true for anyone who will follow these words of Jesus. "Pray always, that you may come off conqueror; yea, that you may conquer Satan, and that you may escape the hands of the servants of Satan that do uphold his work." (D&C 10:5.)

We need not think that we are immune to the devil and his hosts. Regardless of who we are or where we live the old devil would like to have us. The more righteous one is the greater the prize he would be for Satan. For this reason the Lord has also counseled in modern times that the whole Church should take heed and pray always, for, says he, "Yea, and even let those who are sanctified take heed also." (*Ibid.*, 20:34.)

And probably this is illustrated best of all where the Lord addresses his counsel directly to the Prophet Joseph Smith and says, "What I say unto one I say unto all; pray always lest that wicked one have power in you, and remove you out of your place." (*Ibid.*, 93:49.)

From these scriptures we see that the Lord has continually counseled men to pray and promised them that if they will heed that advice they will have a shield of protection against the adversary they can obtain in no other way.

(2) Forgiveness.

From ancient time to the present we have promises from God that he will be merciful to the man who confesses his sins, or that he will forgive the man who confesses his sins and forsakes them.

In Proverbs we find, "He that covereth his sins shall not prosper: but whoso confesseth and forsaketh them shall have mercy." (Proverbs 28:13.)

The apostles of the Lord also taught the same thing; for example, in one New Testament passage we find that "If we confess our sins, he is faithful and just to forgive us our sins, and to cleanse us from all unrighteous." (1 John 1:9.)

A very significant and beautiful illustration of forgiveness of sins by prayer and confession is found in the Book of Mormon. After King Benjamin delivered his great sermon his people were very penitent. They prayed aloud as

. . . with one voice, saying: O have mercy, and apply the atoning blood of Christ that we may receive forgiveness of our sins, and our hearts may be purified; for we believe in Jesus Christ, the Son of God, who created heaven and earth, and all things; who shall come down among the children of men.

And it came to pass that after they had spoken these words the Spirit of the Lord came upon them, and they were filled with joy, having received a remission of their sins, and having peace of conscience, because of the exceeding faith which they had in Jesus Christ who should come. . . . (Mosiah 4:2-3.)

In this passage we discover not only that the people prayed, confessed their sins, and professed belief in Jesus Christ, but also that "they were filled with joy" because they "received a remission of their sins." Furthermore, the scripture explicitly states that those good people had "peace of conscience," the great gift of which we have already spoken.

We should also know that in modern revelation, the Lord has said much concerning this matter. Carefully consider these verses:

Behold, he who has repented of his sins, the same is forgiven, and I, the Lord, remember them no more.

By this ye may know if a man repenteth of his sins—behold, he will confess them and forsake them. (D&C 58:42-43; see also *ibid.*, 61:2; 64:7; 84:61.)

So, here we find another glorious gift which men can enjoy if they will pray. If they do pray always, with real intent, confessing their sins, and forsaking their sins, they will have the strength to overcome them and do them no more, and will receive the precious gift of forgiveness and enjoy "peace of conscience."

(3) Faith and Testimony.

The scriptures teach us that faith is a gift of God, that it is a gift within the reach of all men. But, it, like all things of value, has a price: not a price measured in dollars and cents, but one measured in sincere desire, real intent, integrity of purpose, a price that can be paid only by one's mind, heart, and spirit. The formula for obtaining the gift is the same as the formula for obtaining the price of the gift. One must be willing to acknowledge to himself that he is not self-sufficient. He must recognize his own present weaknesses and limitations. And upon realizing these things he must be humble enough also to acknowledge these things to his Father in heaven. If he will do this with real intent, as has been suggested, he will find that his mind, heart, and spirit will soon detect the seeds of faith growing within his soul. If he continues to nurture those seeds of faith they will grow and develop and be the means of yielding knowledge, powers, and other blessings beyond one's ability to dream. (See Alma 32:26-43.)

(4) Guidance of the Holy Ghost and some of its accompanying blessings.

In this dispensation the Lord has made glorious promises to his people if they will keep his commandments. Attempt to consider the magnitude of this promise: "Pray always, and I will pour out my Spirit upon you, and great shall be your blessing—yea, even more than if you should obtain treasures of earth and corruptibleness to the extent thereof." (D&C 19:38.)

In another place the Lord informs us that it is not just the *praying always*, or as we sometimes say of other things in common parlance, "going through the motions" of prayer, that will bring those great blessings. But it is the "prayer of faith" one must utter, for says the Lord, "And the Spirit shall be given unto you by the prayer of faith. . . ." (*Ibid.*, 42:14.)

By the prayer of faith men can receive unlimited blessings. One of the specific blessings promised the Church is that "by the prayer of your faith ye shall receive my law, that ye may know how to govern my church and have all things right before me." (*Ibid.*, 41: 3.) Later the revelation found in Section 42 of the Doctrine and Covenants was received containing the promised law.

Ponder this promise given to the Prophet Joseph

Smith, if he would ask for it in prayer. "And if thou wilt inquire, thou shalt know mysteries which are great and marvelous; therefore thou shalt exercise thy gift, that thou mayest find out mysteries, that thou mayest bring many to the knowledge of the truth, yea, convince them of the error of their ways." (*Ibid.*, 6:11.)

True it is that he was a Prophet among men, but all of the faithful have been given similar promises by the Lord; for example, on one occasion some of the elders had experienced difficulty in trying to give an understanding of the gospel to their inquirers. A revelation was given to them through the Prophet Joseph Smith. Among other things they were promised that should they call upon the name of the Lord, the Comforter would "teach them all things that are expedient for them—" and that they should pray always that they would not faint, "and inasmuch as they do this," said the Lord, "I will be with them even unto the end." (*Ibid.*, 75:10-11.) How much greater blessing can there be than to have the Lord with you even unto the end?

There are numerous places where the Lord names great blessings of the Holy Ghost one can receive through prayer. Certainly one of the most significant promises for every Latter-day Saint or anyone seriously investigating the gospel is found in the last chapter of the Book of Mormon. The verses are addressed particularly to the reader of the book.

And when ye shall receive these things, I would exhort you that ye would ask God, the Eternal Father, in the name of Christ, if these things are not true; and if ye shall ask with a sincere heart, with real intent, having faith in Christ, he will manifest the truth of it unto you, by the power of the Holy Ghost.

And by the power of the Holy Ghost ye may know the truth of all things. (Moroni 10:4-5.)

That promise is not restricted to time, place, nationality, or race; it is a promise given to all men who will follow its counsel. Notice particularly the comprehensiveness of the last sentence, "And by the power of the Holy Ghost ye may know the truth of *all things*." (Italics ours.)

From the scriptures enumerated here we can see that the promise of the Spirit to men if they would offer the prayer of faith involves not one but many blessings. O how we would humble ourselves, live righteously, and offer prayers of faith, if we could only begin to comprehend the extent and glory of these blessings.

II. *Social Blessings*
(1) Love at Home.

One of the greatest satisfactions a mortal can experience is that of living in a home filled with love. On the other hand, one of the most miserable things that a mortal can endure is having to live in a home devoid of love, one filled with hate, greed, envy, distrust, and the like.

The Lord has made known a cure for the latter, and the means by which love can abound in the home. The beginning of love and the preservation of love in the home is rooted in prayer. The members of the family should pray individually. And if they do have their secret prayers in righteousness their spirits will be so tempered that they will have an influence for good on the other members of the family. But this is not all. There should be family prayer also. In fact, the prophets have counseled us to have family prayers; for example, Amulek, the Book of Mormon prophet, said unto the people: "Cry unto him in your houses, yea over all your household, both morning, mid-day, and evening." (Alma 34:21.) When the Resurrected Lord was among the Nephites, he taught them saying: "Pray in your families unto the Father, always in my name, that your wives and your children may be blessed." (3 Nephi 18:21.)

Just as there are many blessings which can be enjoyed individually through individual secret prayers, there are many blessings which can be obtained through family prayers.

Love at home is a heavenly gift, but mortals can enjoy it if they will seek the Lord in private and family prayers.

(2) Love for Fellow Men.

Another far-reaching blessing which is for some, and can be for all, the result of prayer, is love for fellow men. We recall that when the Savior gave the first great commandment, to love God, he said the second was like unto it. "Thou shalt love thy neighbour as thyself." (Matthew 22:37-39.)

In his Sermon on the Mount he not only taught men to love their neighbors but also to love their enemies. There he said: "Love your enemies, bless them that curse you, do good to them that hate you, and pray for them which despitefully use you, and persecute you." (*Ibid.*, 5:44.)

Within this teaching the Lord reveals a glorious principle. The obvious principle throughout the whole verse is that men should return good for evil, the principle of the golden rule. And through the application of this counsel men through their patience and kindness teach by example the principle of love. But perhaps, even deeper than this, the Lord knew that it is the disposition of fallen man to retaliate and return evil for evil. The real way for one to love his fellow beings is to "bless them," "do good to them," "and pray for them." By this means one does not permit himself to fall into sin, for he learns love instead of hate, and at the same time he creates love for himself in others, therefore ridding them of their hatred. In this, prayer has a cleansing effect, not only upon the one who prays, but also upon the one in whose behalf the prayer is uttered.

Surely love for fellow men is wonderful, and the genuine prayer from the sincere heart promotes this blessing and brings in beneficial returns a hundredfold.

(3) Harmony with Authorities.

The last of what we have chosen to call the social blessings we will consider here is being in harmony with God's authorized servants.

In one of Paul's epistles he says, "I exhort therefore, that, first of all, supplications, prayers, intercessions, and giving of thanks, be made for all men; For kings, *and for all that are in authority. . . .*" (1 Timothy 2:1-2. Italics ours.)

Here the great apostle appeals to his readers to pray for all that are in authority. We are particularly concerned about praying for those who bear God's authority. Those men bear an immeasurable responsibility in the earth and need the prayers of the Saints.

President Joseph F. Smith said, "There never should be a day pass but all the people composing the Church should lift up their voices in prayer to the Lord to sustain his servants who are placed to preside over them." (*GD*:223.)

Not only do God's servants need the blessings which come from the prayers of the Saints, but the Saints need the blessings which will come to them as a result of praying for their leaders. If they pray for their leaders, their souls will be turned more affectionately toward them. They will love them more, and loving them more they will understand them more, and loving them more and understanding them more, they will sustain them more. When one loves the Authorities and sustains the Authorities, he is given a peace and satisfaction of spirit which can come in no way other than being in harmony with God's anointed ones.

Conclusion

In summary, we have seen prayer can be not only communion with God but communication with him. It is a means of man's receiving great blessings, only a very few of which we considered under two general classifications, (1) Personal Blessings, and (2) Social Blessings.

Under Personal Blessings we discussed: (1) Protection against the Adversary, (2) Forgiveness, (3) Faith and Testimony, and (4) Guidance of the Holy Ghost and its Accompanying Blessings.

Under Social Blessings we discussed: (1) Love at Home, (2) Love for Fellow Men, and (3) Harmony with Authorities.

In conclusion let us turn our attention to a promise given by the Lord—a promise every man should always have present in his mind:

> And I say unto you, Ask, and it shall be given you; seek, and ye shall find; knock, and it shall be opened unto you.
>
> For every one that asketh receiveth; and he that seeketh findeth; and to him that knocketh it shall be opened. (Luke 11:9-10.)

Chapter IX

REPENTANCE—THE PRINCIPLE
OF PROGRESSION

Before the Lord began his personal ministry in Palestine, John the Baptist prepared the way for him. The essence of that preparation or of John's message, as recorded by Matthew, was this, "Repent ye: for the kingdom of heaven is at hand." (Matthew 3:2.)

But John was not alone in crying repentance. Mark tells us that "after that John was put in prison, Jesus came into Galilee, preaching the gospel of the kingdom of God, And saying, The time is fulfilled, and the kingdom of God is at hand: repent ye, and believe the gospel." (Mark 1:14-15.)

On one occasion there were some Jews who came to Jesus reporting a rather unusual situation from which they apparently inferred the victims were grievous sinners. The Lord responded to them by saying, "Suppose ye that these Galilaeans were sinners above all the Galilaeans, because they suffered such things? I tell you, Nay: but, except ye repent, ye shall all likewise perish." (Luke 13:2-3.)

In this case the Lord emphatically points out that repentance is not what many or even perhaps most people seem to think it is, something for somebody else, but not for one's self. He makes it clear that a person must be vitally concerned with his own repentance, for he said, "except ye repent, ye shall all likewise perish."

When the Christ had ascended into heaven and the earthly ministry was left in the hands of his disciples, we find that they taught precisely the same doctrine. On the day of Pentecost as Peter preached to the multitude "they were pricked in their heart, and said unto Peter and to the rest of the apostles, Men and brethren, what shall we do? Then Peter said unto them, Repent, and be baptized everyone of you in the name of Jesus Christ for the remission of sins, and ye shall receive the gift of the Holy Ghost." (Acts 2:37-38.)

In our own dispensation the Lord has given revelation upon revelation in which he has bade mankind to repent and instructed his servants to teach repentance. For example, in verses eleven through fourteen of Section 18 of the Doctrine and Covenants, the Lord says, "For, behold, the Lord your Redeemer suffered death in the flesh; wherefore he suffered the pain of all men, that all men might repent and come unto him. And he hath risen again from the dead, that he might bring all men unto him, on conditions of repentance. And how great is his joy in the soul that repenteth! Wherefore, you are called to cry repentance unto this people."

Furthermore, upon examining the scriptures we find that repentance was not only taught by John the Baptist, the Lord Jesus Christ, the apostles of Palestine, and commanded to be taught in our dispensation, but we find that from the very beginning God has called upon men to repent. In the days of Adam ". . . the Lord God called upon men by the Holy Ghost everywhere and commanded them that they should repent; And as many as believed in the Son, and repented of their sins, should be saved; and as many as believed not and repented not, should be damned; and the words went forth out of the mouth of God in a firm decree; wherefore they must be fulfilled." (Moses 5:14-15.)

What is meant by repentance? Quite simply stated it involves three things. First, repentance means forsaking or refraining from doing that which was done which is wrong. Second, repentance means doing that which is right which has been neglected. Third, repentance means making a restitution for offenses where restitution is possible. These are the basic elements of repentance, but they have many implications. Some of the implications of these principles are found in an analysis made by Dr. James E. Talmage. (*AF*:109-112.) His analysis hinges upon two basic ideas, attitude, and action. He names three characteristics which are embodied in the repentant attitude. They are: (1) Conviction of guilt, (2) Desire to be relieved of the hurtful effects of sin, and (3) An earnest determination to forsake sin and do good. These involve no action. They concern the individual and his soul—that is, what happens inside himself. Certainly there would be no disposition to repent if one had no conviction of guilt. After having such a conviction one would then desire to rid himself, and any he had caused to suffer, of the hurtful effects of sin. Then he would make a firm resolve and have an earnest determination to forsake sin and do good. These characteristics reflect the repentant attitude. Yet one who has a repentant attitude cannot be said necessarily to have repented. The attitude is essential to repentance but not repentance itself.

However, the repentant attitude should be the efficient cause, or provide the motivation for the action which produces repentance. Returning to Dr. Talmage a moment, within the idea of action he lists three steps which one must take to have repented, and to obtain forgiveness and a remission of sins. The steps are: (1) Confess sins to God and others who are concerned, (2) Forgive others of their offenses, and (3) Demonstrate confidence in the atoning sacrifice of the Lord by complying with his commandments. These three steps are distinguished from the former in that they require action. They are not reflections or reasonings, desires or resolves, determinations or feelings. They are doings. They involve his doing things. He must confess his sins to the Lord and seek his forgiveness. He must seek forgiveness from those whom he has offended by acknowledging his guilt. And he should seek those whom God has chosen to be judges in his kingdom.

Not only should one confess his sins and solicit a forgiveness of them, but he must forgive others of their offenses. He cannot expect a forgiveness of his sins if he is unwilling to forgive others of theirs.

And the summation of the process of repentance is found in keeping God's commandments. For he who does what God has commanded demonstrates that he not only has a repentant attitude but that he has repented indeed, and accepts the atoning sacrifice of the Lord and loves the Lord, for Jesus said, "If ye love me, keep my commandments." (John 14:15.)

One may ask the question, why is repentance necessary to salvation? Basically, and functionally, for the reason that repentance is the principle of progress. If one had the faith, the knowledge, the will, the love, and the purity which is necessary always to think, and say, and do the right thing, he would have nothing of which he needed to repent. However, experience and revelation both teach us that few mortals, if any, have reached such a condition.

In the broadest terms the word "repentance" has this same application. Whenever a person is doing anything wrong, or incorrectly, or in a less efficient way than it might be done, and discovers his error, or the better way, and then follows it, he applies the principle of repentance; for example, should an engineer do a mathematical problem and make a miscalculation, his error might cause a tragedy on the building or bridge or other structure he is planning. Should he or a colleague discover the error, he would correct it. He would be considered worse than foolish if he did not. And, his correcting the error is a demonstration of the principle of repentance.

This same idea applies to the scientist or technician in the laboratory, to the craftsman in the use of his tools, to the seamstress in the use of her skill, to the surgeon in the operating room, and to all men and women in the performance of their labors in the world. When anyone forsakes a wrong thing or way, for the right or better thing or way he is applying the principle of repentance. Certainly we must agree that this is an extremely practical procedure. In fact, it is the only procedure by which progress can be made.

If we will but consider the matter, we will realize that the idea we have been discussing is one of the basic factors in modern science. At the outset that may seem to be a very strange and perhaps even paradoxical thought that repentance has some relation to science— modern science. Repentance as a concept has always had such a deep and integral connection with religion, and religion and science are not always regarded as being on the best of terms with each other; so it is a rather natural reaction to be perhaps at least a little startled at the suggestion that repentance is a basic factor in modern science. Well, then, what do we mean by this assertion?

Fundamentally, this is our meaning. Our whole structure of modern science with the great knowledge and multitude of advantages it has brought to man is founded on the principle of examining and testing things to see if they will work. If hypotheses fail, new ones are suggested, and the procedure is repeated. And the process does not stop at this point. Researchers and technicians are constantly searching and experimenting in order to make still further advances and improvements. This entire procedure is based on or consistent with (although perhaps unwittingly) the religious teaching of Paul, wherein he said, "Prove all things; hold fast that which is good." (1 Thessalonians 5:21.) Now—

obviously the proving of all things, the dismissing the evil, or that which fails, or that which is inadequate, and the holding fast that which is good is precisely what happens in the operation called repentance. Furthermore, this is also precisely what occurs in modern science as conscientious men and women eagerly strive to make new discoveries and developments in the fields of their particular training and interest. So we see the principle of repentance does have a place in modern science although its usual religious connotations would not immediately suggest it.

In fact we should go much further into this analysis, for actually it has been the operation of this principle which perhaps most clearly distinguishes modern science from ancient science, and likewise is one of the most basic reasons, if not the most basic reason, why modern science has become what it is, has made the almost incredible contribution it has, and has inspired the confidence of millions.

Ancient science was primarily descriptive in nature. The natural philosopher, as he was called, would observe the world, or the universe, or nature, or any of her parts, and then give a report of what he saw, and that was science. He was not a manipulator or experimenter. On the contrary, the modern scientist is an experimenter. He is not satisfied to be a passive observer of his environment. He observes things in the world then formulates hypotheses and finds some way to verify them through experimentation.

In this process he employs the principle of repentance. For through his researches he finds errors or inaccuracies in former conclusions and corrects them, or he finds better ways of doing things, and provides the means whereby the improved methods, devices, and instruments may supplant the former and poorer ones.

To be more concrete and quite specific, let us cite a very significant example. The great Greek philosopher Aristotle, who lived in the fourth century before Christ, claimed that heavy bodies fall faster than light bodies. Because of the great esteem in which Aristotle was held, and far more basically, because apparently no one was of the disposition or inclination to doubt that he was correct and to experiment with falling bodies to find out whether he was right or wrong, the world accepted his opinion on the matter until the seventeenth century of our era. For almost two thousand years his opinion had been accepted primarily for the simple reason that no one tested the opinion to see if it was correct.

But in the seventeenth century there lived a man who wondered about Aristotle's conclusion and devised a means of testing it to see if it were true. Upon examination, experimentation, he discovered that Aristotle was wrong. As significant as that discovery and the consequent mathematical formulations were, that which was of the utmost significance was the fact that experimental method was born. Galileo had awakened the world to the tool which was to be instrumental in wresting from nature many of her secrets, and the process goes on.

Now the point of all the foregoing is this; as long as men only observed and recorded their observations there was no progress or development in science. On the contrary, immediately when men began to apply the principles which they thought about, progress was the result. But it was not merely the application of principles which produced modern science, but it was the dismissing of those things which were not verified, eliminating that which was not confirmed or found to be true or productive of worthy and profitable consequences, and the holding fast that which was good. And thus the progress which has been and is being made by modern science is fundamentally based upon this principle of proving all things and holding fast that which is good; and obviously from what has been stated previously, it is clear that this very process is basically that of repentance, wherein the searcher turns from that which is faulty or inadequate or untrue to that which can stand the test, endure, and produce. So we see that the best possible illustration of progress that we experience (that of modern science) has been possible because of the application of the principle of repentance. Thus when we speak of repentance as the principle of progress, we need not restrict it to a theological or religious context, for we see that it is applicable to all of the affairs of life.

Now for a moment, let us return to the question, why is repentance necessary to salvation?

When it comes to the matter of the salvation of the souls of men, we find that repentance performs identically the same function that it does in areas of other application. That is, when one forsakes thoughts, words, and practices which are inconsistent with the revelations of God, and does things which God has commanded that one should do, he progresses in that he purifies himself and frees himself from a multitude of things which formerly held him in bondage, things which bring pain, suffering, dissension, frustration, distress, sorrow, and regret. And far worse than any one of these, or any combination of them in this life, is the incalculable loss that one would net eternally.

The Lord has said that no unclean thing can dwell in his presence. (See D&C 94:8-9; 97:15-17.) Each person will receive a glory in which there is law that he can abide. For the Lord said, "And Zion cannot be built up unless it is by the principles of the law of the celestial kingdom; otherwise I cannot receive her unto myself." (*Ibid.*, 105:5.) And in another place, ". . . he who is not able to abide the law of a celestial kingdom cannot abide a celestial glory." (*Ibid.*, 88:22.) These scriptures make it evident that in order for one to receive the highest glory he will have to learn and live the highest law. From this we see that repentance is necessary for salvation by virtue of the fact that men do not now abide by the celestial law; throngs do not abide even a lesser law, and they must turn from their ways to obtain salvation, for the word "salvation" itself means to be saved from, or spared, the consequences of ill actions, etc. Repentance then is to forsake the worse for the better.

In Section 130 of the Doctrine and Covenants there are two verses which are significant here. They read:

Whatever principle of intelligence we attain unto in this life, it will rise with us in the resurrection.

And if a person gains more knowledge and intelligence in this life through his diligence and obedience than another, he will have so much the advantage in the world to come. (Verses 18-19.)

I would like to emphasize the use of the words "knowledge" and "intelligence" in these verses. It appears to me that it is not inappropriate to suggest that these words may be distinguished by regarding knowledge as being of a passive or static nature whereas intelligence is active or dynamic. That would mean knowledge is inert of itself, an instrument to be used. Intelligence would be a combination of factors which we might quite simply call disposition or character. This would imply that the disposition or character would determine the use to which the knowledge would be put. Now to paraphrase the scripture in terms of this analysis we find that whatever principle of character (or disposition) we develop or acquire in this life, that is the character (or disposition) we will have in the resurrection. (See also Alma 34:34-35.) And if a person gains more knowledge and intelligence (or good character, or disposition, or love of righteousness) in this life through his diligence and obedience than another, he will have so much the advantage in the world to come.

This also points up the grave importance of repenting of one's sins and shortcomings, for we make of ourselves what we will. All that we think, say, and do not only determines what our knowledge is, but even more important, determines our attitude, our disposition, our character, in short, our intelligence. And now is the time to do something about our sins. No one else can repent for us. Each must do his own repenting. Just as each will progress and be judged according to his knowledge and intelligence, as Section 130 puts it, or to state it differently, according to his knowledge, faith, and works, so at this very moment each is retrogressing, or idling, or progressing, according to his knowledge, faith, and works. Each one should examine himself now, and make a firm resolve that he will repent of his sins or shortcomings and permit himself to progress and become the person he is capable of becoming.

One prophet has said: ". . . do not procrastinate the day of your repentance . . ." (Alma 34:33.) Certainly that is wise counsel. Does procrastination increase or decrease one's ability to repent? What has been your experience? Does your disposition and will to repent increase with procrastination? Or, does it decrease?

Another aspect of procrastination is this. The Lord says, ". . . I the Lord cannot look upon sin with the least degree of allowance; Nevertheless, he that repents and does the commandments of the Lord shall be forgiven; And he that repents not from him shall be taken even the light which he has received; for my Spirit shall not always strive with man." (D&C 1:31-33.) When his Spirit is gone, repentance becomes an impossibility.

The more one does the wrong thing, the greater becomes the barrier between him and God. And remember, God does not build the barrier; the one who sins builds it. In fact the more one does a wrong thing the less freedom he has not to do it. And by the same token, the more he overcomes and does not yield to that temptation, the more freedom he has. In this way one determines the degree of his own freedom. Every time he makes the right choice he increases his freedom, and every time he makes the wrong choice he lessens or decreases his freedom. In this process also we see a connection between repentance and freedom, for when one rejects the evil and accepts the good, it is a manifestation of repentance, and through it he increases his freedom.

In conclusion let us say: remember, repentance has been taught from the beginning, and repentance is a principle which is applicable to all things that we do and say and not just to those we might consider as having religious or spiritual implications. In all of those areas, as well as in the religious area, repentance is the principle of progress. In fact the gospel itself is a plan for improvement. And the inherent concomitant of improvement is freedom.

Chapter X

AN APPROACH TO THE MORMON CONCEPT OF
THE NATURE OF MAN

In one of his addresses at the Utah Conference on Higher Education in 1959 Dr. Philip Wheelwright distinguished three basic types of philosophic orientation for considering the nature of man. These types of orientation are: the theocentric, the anthropocentric, and the physiocentric. I do not recall Dr. Wheelwright's having designated the theocentric view by any other name, although he did call the anthropocentric view humanism and the physiocentric view pure naturalism. He considered the theocentric and physiocentric views as extremes with the anthropocentric view as the mean. Perhaps he arranged the three views in that order for that reason. But his arrangement might also be used to suggest that the physical orientation is the lowest, the human orientation is higher, and the divine orientation is highest. In this scheme the anthropocentric view subsumes the physiocentric view, and similarly the theocentric view subsumes the anthropocentric view. That is to say, the theocentric view is the most inclusive, for it transcends not only the physical world but mortal man also, and therefore no ultimate values contained in the other two perspectives are lost in this perspective.

In Dr. Wheelwright's terminology the Mormon concept of man is theocentric. That is, the nature of man cannot be understood devoid of knowledge of man's relationship to God. Traditionally, although frequently only poetically or metaphorically, man has spoken of God anthropomorphically and even, we claim that God is an anthropomorphic being. Of course, the point *we* attempt to stress with those claims, fundamentally, is that God is a tangible being, in the same *generic* form as man. However, inasmuch as our form derives from him, and our ultimate form is to be eternally tabernacled like him, I think it would be more accurate to say man is a theomorphic being rather than say God is an anthropomorphic being. Another way of stating it is to say man is of the race of the Gods rather than say God is of the race of men. Inasmuch as man is the off-spring of God and his life is not merely of mortal duration, one can hardly expect to understand accurately man's nature if these things are ignored.

Now, what do I mean by the nature of man? I will consider this briefly in terms of four questions. First, what is man? Second, what is his state or condition? Third, what are his characteristics? And fourth, what is he potentially?

Now first, what is man? The Lord has revealed that man as mortal has three determinate aspects to his being: intelligence, spirit, and body. Each man's original being, called an intelligence, was provided a tabernacle of substance called spirit. Spirit beings in turn are tabernacled in bodies of flesh. A mortal man, or soul, is thus a union of spirit and body. Therefore, man is a being who has both mortal and immortal parents, for his body is provided for him through the physical processes involved in procreation, and his spirit is provided by celestial parents. In considering the nature of man, therefore, we must at least be cognizant that man has more than a mere biological heritage from mortals. He also has a life-heritage from celestial parents plus whatever capacities, talents, and dispositions he may have developed in his pre-mortal existence.

Second, what is man's state or condition? As before stated, we call man's condition mortal. Simply, this means that man is subject to death. Not only is he subject to death but also to sin. Fundamentally this subjection of man is what is meant by saying he is in a fallen state. Different philosophies call man's situation by different names, but universally, I believe, it is regarded as a predicament.

Third, what are man's characteristics? This question, its answers, and their implications are probably what is intended or meant by most people when they ask what is the nature of man? In typical familiar words men are honest, true, chaste, benevolent, virtuous, etc.; but they are also dishonest, false, unchaste, malevolent, vicious, and so on. Man is a rational being, as the philosophers have trumpeted through the centuries, but he is also an irrational being, as some have reluctantly admitted since Plato, and others have widely and loudly proclaimed in the last century. Man is an egoist, as Hobbes vigorously declared, but he is also an altruist, as Shaftesbury, Hume, Kant, and Mill maintain in various ways. Or in Martin Buber's words, which were used *ad nauseam* in the conference mentioned above, man extensively finds himself in an I-It relationship, but it is possible for him also to know the I-Thou relationship. And as also was suggested in the conference, but not stated in the explicit language of social psychology, man does make decisions under the conscious or unconscious influence of reference groups.

As man is observed, his conduct does not reveal a simple continuum from vice to virtue, but a vast complex in which each man manifests some combination of virtues and vices.

Fourth, what is man's potentiality? In a modern revelation the Lord says:

Every spirit of man was innocent in the beginning; and God having redeemed man from the fall, men became again, in their infant state, innocent before God. (D&C 93:38.)

There are several fascinating ideas here, but the point I want to make is that as each spirit enters its body of flesh in the infant state it is innocent before God.

The revelation continues:

And that wicked one cometh and taketh away light and truth, through disobedience, from the children of men, and because of the tradition of their fathers. (*Ibid.*, 93:39.)

There are two points I wish to draw from this verse. First, the wicked one, the devil, "cometh and taketh away light and truth." And second, he does this through man, individually and collectively—individually through disobedience and collectively through the tradition of their fathers.

Essentially, one of the significant things this means is that infants are innocent, but they are born in a mortal world where men are agents unto themselves, even acknowledging various influences which may contribute to decision-making, and where, through the exercise of agency, men individually have chosen in varying degrees to acknowledge or deny God and similarly have chosen to accept and practice or reject his principles in varying degrees. Consequently, although babes are innocent, by the time they reach the age of accountability they have become acquainted, through personal weaknesses and those of others, with a fallen world. Although not comprehending these words, they no doubt quite adequately understand that man has his failings. Perhaps this is in part what King Benjamin had in mind when he said:

For the natural man is an enemy to God, and has been from the fall of Adam, and will be, forever and ever, unless he yields to the enticings of the Holy Spirit, and putteth off the natural man and becometh a saint through the atonement of Christ the Lord, and becometh as a child, submissive, meek, humble, patient, full of love, willing to submit to all things which the Lord seeth fit to inflict upon him, even as a child doth submit to his father. (Mosiah 3:19.)

Another passage speaks of the natural man as carnal, sensual, and devilish. Let me hasten to say it is probably impossible for us even to guess what the corrupt state of man would be had there not been periodic restorations of the gospel in man's history and some glimmer of spiritual knowledge trickling down through the centuries. However, I must also say, and emphatically, this is not identical by any means with the apostate Christian doctrine of depravity.

As I examine the scriptures it appears to me that the words "carnal," "sensual," and "devilish," must not be limited to their more narrow and specific connotations, but they are accurately, though more broadly, interpreted by the scriptural phrase "enemy to God." That is, not all men who have not made the covenants with the Christ are given to indulging in practices which are appropriately designated carnal, sensual, and devilish. Yet, all men, regardless of how moral and how pure they may be with reference to those practices called carnal, sensual, and devilish, are enemies to God until they yield to the enticings of the Holy Spirit, accept the atonement of the Lord, and are submissive to his will. A significant point here is, what we conventionally call basic personal and social morality are not enough. For one not to be an enemy to God he must do all things whatsoever the Lord his God shall command him. (See Abraham 3:25.)

So, man comes into the world innocent; he is free and purposive. He seeks self-preservation and self-fulfillment. He encounters thwartings because of his own nature, his environment, and the cosmic process. The thwartings produce antagonisms and frustrations. Antagonisms and frustrations possibly provoke man to sin. A product of sin is guilt, and probably more frustration and need for self-assertion. Guilt in turn often leads to despair. Through it all the sense of fulfillment may at some point become perverted. Or, on the other hand, man may be able to cope with his thwartings and frustrations, sins, feelings of guilt, etc., and be a noble example of mortality at its unredeemed best. But not only does man have the mortal potentialities suggested here but also available to him is his highest ultimate potentiality of becoming in character like his celestial parents.

In summary, then, the Mormon concept of the nature of man may be called theocentric. Man is a son of God as well as a son of man. He has a celestial life-heritage as well as a biological heritage. He has capacities, talents, and dispositions developed in his pre-mortal state. At present he is a mortal or fallen being, subject to sin and death. He has the agency to choose between virtues and vices. He comes into this world innocent, with a potentiality ranging from a son of perdition to a celestial being. The biological and social sciences and some other disciplines can, should, and do illumine our understandings of the nature of man. But in order that they may illumine, and not obscure our understanding, we must strive to comprehend what the Lord has revealed. If we focus all of our attention on fallen man, perhaps we will have difficulty ever rising above fallen man. Perhaps due consideration to both fallen man and potentially celestial man will result in our being acceptable to the redeeming power of the Lord.

Chapter XI

FREE AGENCY AND
PSYCHIC DETERMINISM

The Lord gave Abraham a great vision in which he was shown the intelligences that were organized before the world was. (Abraham 3:22.) The Lord said: ". . . I rule in the heavens above, and in the earth beneath, in all wisdom and prudence, over all the intelligences thine eyes have seen from the beginning; I came down in the beginning in the midst of all the intelligences thou hast seen." (*Ibid.*, 3:21.) It appears Abraham was shown all the intelligences which were organized before the world was, intelligences which were to come to this world, but that there were other intelligences which Abraham was not shown. Abraham was told the intelligences have no beginning; ". . . they existed before, they shall have no end, they shall exist after, for they are gnolaum, or eternal." (*Ibid.*, 3:18.)

The same concept was revealed to Joseph Smith as follows: "Man was also in the beginning with God. Intelligence, or the light of truth, was not created or made, neither indeed can be." (D&C 93:29.) The original state of man was that of an intelligence. Furthermore, intelligences, like truth, are independent in the spheres in which God places them, to act for themselves; otherwise, says the revelation, there is no existence. (See *ibid.*, 93:30.) This is a simple and clear statement of the principle of idealistic metaphysics that essentially if there were no minds there would be no existence, for irrespective of what physical phenomena actually existed, that existence would be fundamentally the same as non-existence if there were no minds to perceive or imagine them.

Not only does the Lord inform us that intelligences are eternal and have the power to act for themselves, but he tells us that they were innocent in the beginning, and because of the redemption from the fall men again became innocent in their infant state. (*Ibid.*, 93:38.)

It is a fact of observation that even infants with the same parents very early manifest diverse tendencies, desires, and aversions and on the basis of the revelations of the Lord it is not unreasonable to make the inferences that each infant that comes into the world was an entity—an intelligence, a spirit, a personality—prior to entering the body provided for it through the process of procreation, and likewise possesses its own common and unique proclivities in addition to whatever biological characteristics it may have inherited from its mortal forebearers.

Although little children have their differences, their own likes and dislikes, God has revealed ". . . that little children are redeemed from the foundation of the world through . . . [his] Only Begotten; Wherefore, they cannot sin, for power is not given unto Satan to tempt little children, until they begin to become accountable before . . ." the Lord. (*Ibid.*, 29:46-47.) Apparently, even though little children are subject to many influences, and do some things which might be regarded as sin if done by one more mature than they, in the justice and mercy of God they are not held accountable for their deeds until they reach an age at which they should be able to discern between good and evil.

As children manifest their likes and dislikes they reveal what we have come to call the power of choice. The Prophet Lehi suggests, as do others, that there is eternal law (generically speaking), and that eternal beings—intelligences, spirits, mortals, post-mortal spirits, resurrected beings—by virtue of the fact that they are intelligences, inherently have the power to act contrary to the law. Conforming to the law constitutes righteousness and yields happiness, and acting in opposition to the law constitutes sin and yields misery.

Further, Lehi says: "And the Messiah cometh in the fulness of time, that he may redeem the children of men from the fall. And because that they are redeemed from the fall they have become free forever, knowing good from evil; to act for themselves and not to be acted upon, save it be by the punishment of the law at the great and last day, according to the commandments which God hath given. Wherefore, men are free according to the flesh; and all things are given them which are expedient unto man. And they are free to choose liberty and eternal life, through the great mediation of all men, or to choose captivity and death, according to the captivity and power of the devil; for he seeketh that all men might be miserable like unto himself." (2 Nephi 2:26-27.)

In effect Lehi says: Because of the fall all men were in captivity to the devil, but because of the atonement of the Messiah, men have become free to act for themselves and not to be acted upon unless they fail to observe God's commandments.

That man has the power to act and is responsible for his actions is made very clear by the Lord through the Prophet Joseph Smith in these words: "For behold, it is not meet that I should command in all things; for he that is compelled in all things, the same is a slothful and not a wise servant; wherefore he receiveth no reward. Verily I say, men should be anxiously engaged in a good cause, and do many things of their own free will, and bring to pass much righteousness; For the power is in them, wherein they are agents unto themselves. And inasmuch as men do good they shall in nowise lose their reward. But he that doeth not anything until he is commanded, and receiveth a commandment with doubtful heart, and keepeth it with slothfulness, the same is damned." (D&C 58:26-29.)

As law is eternal, and agency is eternal, opposition seems also to be eternal. The scriptures indicate that in the pre-mortal existence spirits had the power to act in opposition to God and eternal law even to the point of rebellion. In this mortal existence even as the light of Christ or Holy Spirit enlighteneth every man who comes into the world and will respond to its influence, similarly the influence of the adversary is present to beguile and deceive men and lead them carefully down to hell.

The Lord has said that the devil takes away light and truth from the children of men in two ways, generically speaking. First, by the disobedience of men they lose the truth, and secondly, through the traditions of their fathers. (*Ibid.*, 93:39.) One is held accountable only for the light and truth he receives or has opportunity to receive. If he is born in an environment where he has access to the full light of the gospel, his responsibility will be different from that of the person who is born in an environment devoid of that light. However, where one does not have access to the full light of the gospel if he is faithful and persists in the light he has with full purpose of heart he shall receive more light, but either in this life or in the post-mortal life every man will have opportunity to responsibly accept or reject the light, even as one third of the hosts of heaven made their final choice even in the pre-mortal estate.

Now the Lord has said that all blessings are predicated upon law. Through the Prophet Joseph Smith he revealed that "There is a law, irrevocably decreed in heaven before the foundations of this world, upon which all blessings are predicated—And when we obtain any blessing from God, it is by obedience to that law upon which it is predicated." (*Ibid.*, 130:20-21.) Perhaps it is not unwarranted to assume that by implication there is not only a loss of blessings but even disvalues or definite handicaps or disadvantages which come to man upon the disobedience of laws.

Regarding the binding nature of law, the Lord has said, "I, the Lord, am bound when ye do what I say; but when ye do not what I say, ye have no promise." (*Ibid.*, 82:10.)

Law, then, seems to be not only eternal, and the basis of all blessings, and the loss of blessings, and binding upon God as well as man, but according to God is also universal. He has revealed: "All kingdoms have a law given; And there are many kingdoms; for there is no space in the which there is no kingdom; and there is no kingdom in which there is no space, either a greater or a lesser kingdom. And unto every kingdom is given a law; and unto every law there are certain bounds also and conditions." (*Ibid.*, 88:36-38.) In spite of the obvious disorder and apparent chaos and meaninglessness of part and in some cases even much of man's existence, God has assured us that space and its vast continuum of kingdoms are governed by law and that each law has its own bounds and conditions.

According to Lehi the whole cosmic order is designed that man might have joy. (2 Nephi 2:25.) The ultimate realization of that joy (or its opposite, misery) seems to depend upon man's use of his agency, or power to act. Although, because of the redemption, he comes into this world innocent, he does not remain innocent because of the fact that as he grows and develops physically, his intellectual, emotional, and volitional aspects develop also, and through them he makes choices. If he chooses to yield to the enticings of the Holy Spirit, and puts off the natural man and becomes a saint through the atonement of Christ the Lord, and becomes as a child, submissive, meek, humble, patient, full of love, willing to submit to all things which the Lord sees fit to inflict upon him, even as a child submits to his father, then he is blessed and will find himself a new man who is happy and an heir to all the Father has. (See Mosiah 3:19.) If he rejects the enticings of the Holy Spirit and chooses darkness rather than light he receives captivity and death (misery) or whatever level of joy he is willing to receive, for the Lord has revealed that even after they have been resurrected who will go even to the lowest degree of glory "they who remain shall also be quickened; nevertheless, they shall return again to their own place, to enjoy that which they are willing to receive, because they were not willing to enjoy that which they might have received." (D&C 88:32.)

Now that we have had a brief doctrinal statement regarding man and his agency let us specifically examine what might be called free agency and psychic determinism. First, what do we mean by the phrases "free agency" and "psychic determinism"? Based upon the foregoing and particularly verses 29 through 31 of Section 93 of the Doctrine and Covenants I would define free agency as the power to act for itself inherent in intelligence (or in an intelligence). I define psychic determinism as the hypothesis that all of an intelligence's choices are irrevocably determined from the pristine existence of the intelligence by the nature of that particular intelligence.

Although free agency is defined in terms of power to act, implicit in the notion of intelligence is the power to discern. One's condemnation, therefore, lies not merely in the fact of his wrong choice but also in the fact that he had the power to discern and discerning made the wrong choice. As it is put in one place:

"Behold, here is the agency of man, and here is the condemnation of man; because that which was from the beginning is plainly manifest unto them, and they receive not the light. And every man whose spirit receiveth not the light is under condemnation." (*Ibid.*, 93: 31-32.)

As mentioned above, adults observe many discernible differences in children from their infancy. They are distinct persons when they are born, though innocent as far as this world is concerned, having made no choices here. Far more important than any biological factors which may have contributed to their being what they are are the attributes of character which they develop by their own volition as beings in their pre-mortal existence. So, though they are all innocent as regards this life when they are born they are by no means all alike. Obviously, neither are the environments of their birth and nurturing alike. The factors which influence each individual from infancy to old age are many and varied. Among them are the following: parents, brothers and sisters, other relatives, friends, members of one's peer group, teachers, neighbors, things seen, heard, and read, the things one is taught and the manner in which he is taught, the extent of his education, jobs had and things related thereto, his hopes, disappointments, aspirations, successes, concept of self, and what he thinks others think of him, etc.

It is beyond the ken of man to say categorically what constitutes an ideal set of circumstances for a given infant. We must assume that each is born into a set of mortal circumstances appropriate to whatever he became in the pre-mortal existence. Viewing temporal conditions as they are and the lives of men and women I think we must conclude that what might be an ideal set of circumstances for one worthy and deserving spirit may be radically different from those of another worthy and deserving spirit. There is no justification for one's considering those born in less favorable temporal circumstances than his own as necessarily spiritually inferior to him or those born in more favorable temporal circumstances than his own as necessarily spiritually superior to him. Generally speaking it would appear that some spirits do have a distinct advantage over others because of the environments in which they are reared, and probably generally speaking they are in that environment because it is what they deserved and that which is best for them. However, it is also a probability that some equally deserving and worthy spirits are born in a time and place and under conditions which are far less propitious viewed from our mortal perspective, and yet probably in their interests and perhaps in the interest of others they are so born.

The concept of free agency takes cognizance of these differences and acknowledges the seemingly infinite and varied influences which affect the lives of men. But irrespective of the diversity and multiplicity of those factors which may be operative in the life of a given individual the concept of free agency holds that the individual is not an inert entity pushed to and fro, or molded first this way and then that, either mercilessly or mercifully, by the necessary and inexorable combination of forces which may be operating upon it. On the contrary, the concept of free agency holds that inasmuch as one has intelligence (or basically, is an intelligence), is basically a discerning entity with the power to act, he has the responsibility to examine those things which come within his purview, and irrespective of what combination of influences may be exerted upon him, as a discerning agent, he must assume responsibility for whatever choices he makes. Essentially, whatever the influencing forces, whether construed as coercive or otherwise, the individual is regarded as the deciding agent. It is his inherent responsibility, by virtue of his being an intelligence, to discern and act in accordance with his agency, and accept the responsibility for his choice.

In one place the Lord revealed: "And again, inasmuch as parents have children in Zion, or in any of her stakes which are organized, that teach them not to understand the doctrine of repentance, faith in Christ the Son of the living God, and of baptism and the gift of the Holy Ghost by the laying on of the hands, when eight years old, the sin be upon the heads of the parents." (D&C 68:25.)

This passage clearly places the responsibility for the teaching of children upon their parents. And, as observed above, there are many agents which are either potential or actual influences in the lives of adults as well as children. As agents, all of these persons, as well as parents, are responsible for the influences they exert upon others. In short, agency involves a vast complex of responsibility, essentially involving the responsibility for one's own choices and the influence of those choices upon others.

Undoubtedly the choices one makes in the early stages of his life, along with their consequences, do have their effect in making him whatever kind of person he becomes. But at each stage, or continuously for that matter, one is still a discerner and an agent. If one earnestly and honestly acknowledges the Lord and calls upon him for assistance, he can obtain guidance in the discerning and courage and strength in the acting. If he fails to acknowledge and call upon the Lord he is left to do the best he can and perhaps is influenced in lesser or greater degree by the adversary.

The Lord's admonition in the Sermon on the Mount suggests rather emphatically that one's freedom and responsibility in thinking are basically the same as one's freedom and responsibility in acting. He said: "That whosoever looketh on a woman to lust after her hath

committed adultery with her already in his heart."
(Matthew 5:28.) This perhaps raises the question, is one
going to be judged and held accountable for every idea
or thought which crosses his mind? The answer seems
to require more than a simple yes or no. It has
been said, ". . . As he thinketh in his heart, so is he."
(Proverbs 23:7.)

The Lord in giving instruction to Samuel said regarding a particular man: ". . . Look not on his countenance, or on the height of his stature; because I have
refused him: for the Lord seeth not as man seeth; for
man looketh on the outward appearance, but the Lord
looketh on the heart." (1 Samuel 16:7.) Jesus said to the
Pharisees: "For out of the heart proceed evil thoughts,
murders, adulteries, fornications, thefts, false witness,
blasphemies. . . ." (Matthew 15:19.) More comprehen-
sively the Lord said to the Jews: "O generation of vipers,
how can ye, being evil, speak good things? for out of the
abundance of the heart the mouth speaketh. A good man
out of the good treasure of the heart bringeth forth good
things: and an evil man out of the evil treasure bringeth
forth evil things. But I say unto you, That every idle
word that men shall speak, they shall give account
thereof in the day of judgment." (*Ibid.*, 12:34-36.)
These words from the prophets and the Lord suggest
that it is not the intrusion of a thought in one's mind as
it may be introduced by another, or even the uninvited
flash of a notion in one's mind precipitated or provoked
by any one of a number of things, for which one will be
judged and condemned, but that he will be judged and
condemned for those thoughts which arise out of or
are the product of his heart. Or, he will be judged for
those thoughts which are evil which he contemplates
for whatever sense of base satisfaction he obtains from
them. But what about the Lord's statement, "That every
idle word that men shall speak, they shall give account

thereof in the day of judgment"? Some of the synonyms for the word "idle" will help here. They are: vain, empty, base, having no value or significance, worthless, useless, futile. It appears then that one will be held accountable for the use he makes of his mind in its acts of contemplation as well as in its decisions. The thoughts one entertains not only form the mind but also are a reflection of it. Each intelligence is always the ground of his own choice.

Speaking generally, choices seem to be of three kinds: (1) arbitrary, (2) habitual, and (3) deliberate. By arbitrary I mean such a choice as when one is offered a glass from a tray filled with glasses, or a roll from a plate filled with rolls of the same kind. It is true some persons may pause and even overtly appear to deliberate before choosing, but ultimately such a choice is arbitrary. That is, there is no reason for choosing one rather than another.

By habitual I mean such a choice as when one consistently and almost without thinking always orders milk, or coffee, or some other specific thing as his drink at a given meal or meals.

By deliberate I mean such a choice as when one must decide either to go to hear a symphonic concert played by an orchestra from a remote place, or go to an important basketball game. He cannot go to both, for they are scheduled at the same time.

A given choice may be arbitrary for some persons, habitual for others, and deliberate for still others; for example, if a group of people were given their choice of vanilla or chocolate ice cream, some may be completely indifferent and choose arbitrarily; others may habitually choose one or the other, while still others may deliberately choose one or the other on the basis of what they had previously eaten, or on the basis of what they had the last time they ate ice cream, or for some other definite reason.

Past decisions undoubtedly have bearing on present decisions. Past thoughts and actions, experiences, consequences, reactions of other people, etc., all play their part as one consciously reacts to them or fails to assert his right and responsibility of agency and yields rather indifferently and/or subconsciously to those forces. One is always the agent, although by default he may have submitted himself to subversive influences which in effect may have produced in him a condition of such weakness that he has little confidence in himself and may even feel that he has no power within himself to act. Such a person, fundamentally, is in the state described by Lehi as captivity. But, his captivity does not have to be permanent, if he can be persuaded to assert himself even in a very limited way. From such an assertion of himself he can gain strength which in time may gain for him a full restoration of his agency.

To illustrate the notion of temporary default of agency on an amoral or innocuous level I would suggest the following probably not uncommon experience. One leaves his home driving his automobile with the intent of going to town to make a small purchase. En route he lets his mind wander to a number of things, and suddenly he reaches the intersection where he should turn right in order to go to town where he is to make his purchase. However, when he reaches the intersection instead of turning right he turns left, for he always (so to speak) turns left there in order to go to his office. After he turns or even after he reaches his office, he may or may not remember that it was his intent to go to town rather than directly to his office. This illustrates the fact that sometimes a given pattern of conduct is so strong that even when it is one's intent to follow a different pattern unless he consciously persists in his intent he will find himself doing the usual rather than the intended.

Of course it is on the levels of legal, moral, and religious standards that wrong decisions made consciously or by default weaken and enslave one.

There have been times when good men in high places have compromised or relaxed their standards either momentarily until they came to a sudden awareness of their mistake and fortunately found strength to correct their innovation, or have continued to compromise and make the wrong choices until they have practically made a complete inversion of their standards. But also there have been others who have had a given relatively low standard of conduct, or been given habitually to certain practices for many years who find the strength or power either to gradually or instantaneously forsake those practices and begin to take a more positive and constructive course in their pattern of life.

In either set of circumstances one who has intelligence has the power to consider, the power to discern, and the power to act. He remains responsible for the choices he makes, or for submitting to the particular influence to which he does submit.

There are three large or extensive universal enterprises among men which either explicitly or implicitly assume the reality of the capacity of man to make choices and his responsibility for them. Those enterprises are (1) education, broadly conceived, (2) civil law, and (3) religion, with its concept of rewards and punishments.

First, a word about education. Whether we think of education as that process which takes place in a formal and institutional situation, or as that which happens in the very informal circumstances of home, hogan, or igloo, the process of teaching the infant, small child, larger child, etc., has implicit within it the assumption that the person instructed can understand and make wiser choices because of increased understanding. Also, the entire system of civil law is so conceived that it assumes that men are able to understand laws and make responsible choices. Just as parents punish their children for mistakes in the moral realm on the assumption that the children do or can understand and therefore are responsible, so the civil law provides for punishment for its offenders on the same assumption that they do or can understand, and are responsible. Similarly, the concept of rewards and punishments in religion contains the implicit assumption that men are agents and are responsible for the use of their agency. Certainly the restored gospel is emphatic regarding man's agency and responsibility, the culmination of the exercise of which is assignment to one of the three degrees of glory or perdition.

It is probably also obvious that in what we have here called the enterprise of education, which is basic to the other two enterprises, there is a factor or element which is regarded by many as the cause-effect or deterministic element. It is apparent that fundamental to the process of education, again broadly conceived, is not only the assumption of a capacity to understand and to choose, but also the assumption that concepts conveyed in that process will cause the person to act or choose differently from what he would were he to remain without those concepts.

Since the days of Copernicus and Galileo there has been a progressive development in the area of cause-effect analysis in which the rather thorough-going mechanical characteristics found in or attributed to the physical universe have come to be regarded as equally applicable to the intellectual, emotional, and volitional aspects of man. Needless to say, man, having a body and operating in a corporeal context is involved in cause-effect situations just as any other body, inanimate or animate. That is, should he be outside when it commenced to rain he would become wet just as any other body which happened to be in the rain. But as an agent he may choose to stay in the rain and let the sun and atmosphere dry him later as other bodies, or he may gain shelter from the rain and dry himself. To conclude that inasmuch as man is subject to many cause-effect relationships, as are all bodies, all that he does is mechanical (deterministic) does not take sufficient cognizance of his being a *causer*.

Essentially, the distinction I wish to make may be summarized in the difference between two words, "cause" and "because." The basic concept of cause is *to bring about, to make happen, to effect, to induce, to produce*. The basic concept of because is *for the reason that*, or *on account of*, or *since*, or *inasmuch as*.

Obviously man functions as a cause. However, he also functions in the sense of because. That is, man is not merely moved as effect, which move becomes a cause of a subsequent effect, etc., but because of his intelligence which embodies the power to act, as previously noted, he causes changes *because of* certain things. Those things may be past, present, or future. That is, because of things which have happened he may choose to do a particular thing. Or, because of present circumstances he may choose to act in a particular way. Or, because of a desired or anticipated situation he may act in a given way. Man is not impelled to move this way and that inexorably as an inanimate object or an animate object of a low order, but as he has intelligence he can, and is, responsible to examine any given existential situation and determine what course of action to take. So, his actions are not merely *caused* in a mechanistic or deterministic sense, but as he has the capacity and responsibility to examine any so-called causal factors in any given situation we may suggest that his actions are *becaused*. Irrespective of the number, variety, and nature of the causal factors the individual is the determining factor. And although men in varying degrees may attempt to abdicate their place as agent, they remain unable to shift the final responsibility, either to another agent or to a purported process of inexorable necessity. Therefore, we may say what man does is not merely caused *vis a tergo* (that is, moved by a force from behind), but on the contrary it is becaused *teleologically* (that is, purposively).

As an eternally existing intelligence man had the power to act as God clothed him with spirit and later with mortal body. God has preserved man's freedom to act for himself. In this life man is free to choose either good or evil, but he is *not free from* choosing evil. God also is free to choose good or evil, but different from man he is *free from* choosing evil. It would be wonderful if all men would choose and assist others to choose in such a way that they would exchange their kind of freedom for God's kind of freedom.

Chapter XII

THE GOSPEL AND WORLD RELIGIONS

The revelations of the Lord clearly indicate that Adam was the first man. (TPJS: 167; D&C 84:16; Moses 1:34; Moses 3:7.) As a consequence of the fall, Adam and Eve were cast out of the Garden of Eden, and in time they were blessed with sons and daughters who began to divide two and two and till the land and tend flocks; and they also were blessed with sons and daughters.

Adam and Eve called upon the name of the Lord, and he heard them and gave them commandments to worship him and offer the firstlings of their flocks as an offering unto him. Because of their obedience to the Lord's commandments an angel was sent to Adam and revealed many things to him.

Some of the principles of the gospel with which Adam was acquainted are the following:

(1) Marriage
(2) Faith
(3) Repentance
(4) Baptism
(5) The Holy Ghost
(6) The Fall
(7) The Atonement
(8) Free Agency
(9) Immortality
(10) Revelation
(11) Priesthood

(Hunter, Milton R., *The Gospel Through the Ages* [Salt Lake City: Stevens and Wallis, Inc., 1945], p. 60.)

It is evident from this list, based on the limited revelation we have on the subject, that Adam had an extensive knowledge of the gospel.

Not only was he acquainted with the priesthood, but he held the keys of the priesthood. The Prophet Joseph Smith said:

The Priesthood was first given to Adam; he obtained the First Presidency, and held the keys of it from generation to generation. He obtained it in the Creation, before the world was formed, as in Genesis 1:26, 27, 28. He had dominion given him over every living creature. He is Michael the Archangel, spoken of in the Scriptures. (*TPJS*:157.)

Furthermore, the Prophet said that after an apostasy the keys of authority are restored from heaven by Adam's authority (*ibid.*:157) and that the "... angels are under the direction of Michael or Adam, who acts under the direction of the Lord." (*Ibid.*:168.) Also, the Lord "... set the ordinances to be the same forever and ever, and set Adam to watch over them, to reveal them from heaven to man, or to send angels to reveal them." (*Ibid.*:168.)

Thus, in the words of the Lord:

... the Gospel began to be preached, from the beginning, being declared by holy angels sent forth from the presence of God, and by his own voice, and by the gift of the Holy Ghost. And thus all things were confirmed unto Adam, by an holy ordinance, and the gospel preached, and a decree sent forth, that it should be in the world, until the end thereof; and thus it was. Amen. (Moses 5:58-59.)

Adam and Eve taught the gospel to their sons and daughter, but Satan came among them saying:

Believe it not; and they believed it not, and they loved Satan more than God. And men began from that time forth to be carnal, sensual, and devilish. And the Lord God called upon men by the Holy Ghost everywhere and commanded them that they should repent. (*Ibid.*, 5:13-14.)

In those days mankind generally was referred to as the sons of men. Those who accepted the gospel and made covenants with the Lord were called the sons of God. Thus men and women outside the covenant were the sons and daughters of men, and those who made covenants with the Lord were the sons and daughters of God.

Adam and Eve had a language which was pure and undefiled, and they taught it to their children so they could read and write, and from that time a book of remembrance was kept in the language of Adam; and we are told ". . . for it was given unto as many as called upon God to write by the spirit of inspiration." (*Ibid.*, 6:5.)

One of the greatest meetings in the history of this earth was held when Adam was 927 years of age. Concerning that meeting we are informed:

Three years previous to the death of Adam he called Seth, Enos, Cainan, Mahalaleel, Jared, Enoch, and Methuselah, who were all high priests, with the residue of his posterity who were righteous, into the valley of Adam-ondi-Ahman, and there bestowed upon them his last blessing.

And the Lord appeared unto them, and they rose up and blessed Adam, and called him Michael, the prince, the archangel.

And the Lord administered comfort unto Adam, and said unto him: I have set thee to be at the head; a multitude of nations shall come of thee, and thou art a prince over them forever.

And Adam stood up in the midst of the congregation; and, notwithstanding he was bowed down with age, being full of the Holy Ghost, predicted whatsoever should befall his posterity unto the latest generation. (D&C 107:53-56.)

It is wonderful to contemplate that great meeting where Adam stood before his righteous posterity including the other antediluvian patriarchs and received the Lord in their presence who administered comfort to Adam in his great age. This was a crowning recognition at the end of his mortal life of his faith and devotion.

Throughout Adam's long mortal span the sure knowledge of God was among mankind. In the second "Lecture on Faith" we find these very significant remarks:

. . . after man's transgression . . . [God continued] to manifest himself to him [Adam] and to his posterity; and, notwithstanding they were separated from his immediate presence that they could not see his face, they continued to hear his voice,

Adam, thus being made acquainted with God, communicated the knowledge which he had unto his posterity; and it was through this means that the thought was first suggested to their minds that there was a God, which laid the foundation for the exercise of their faith, through which they could obtain a knowledge of his character and also of his glory.

Not only was there a manifestation made unto Adam of the existence of a God; but Moses informs us, as before quoted that God condescended to talk with Cain after his great transgression in slaying his brother, and that Cain knew that it was the Lord that was talking with him, so that when he was driven out from the presence of his brethren, he carried with him the knowledge of the existence of a God; and, through this means, doubtless, his posterity became acquainted with the fact that such a Being existed.

From this we can see that the whole human family in the early age of their existence, in all their different branches, had this knowledge disseminated among them; so that the existence of God became an object of faith in the early age of the world. (30-33.)

. . . the testimony which these men had of the existence of a God, was the testimony of man; for previous to the time that any of Adam's posterity had obtained a manifestation of God to themselves, Adam, their common father, had testified unto them of the existence of God, and of his eternal power and Godhead. (35.)

From this account [the genealogy of the patriarchs] it appears that Lamech, the 9th from Adam, and the father of Noah, was 56 years old when Adam died; Methuselah, 243; Enoch, 308; Jared, 470; Mahalaleel, 535; Cainan, 605; Enos, 695; and Seth, 800.

So that Lamech the father of Noah, Methuselah, Enoch, Jared, Mahalaleel, Cainan, Enos, Seth, and Adam, were all living at the same time, and beyond all controversy, were all preachers of righteousness. (38-39.)

From the foregoing it is easily to be seen, not only how the knowledge of God came into the world, but upon what principle it was preserved; that from the time it was first communicated, it was retained in the minds of righteous men, who taught not only their own posterity but the world; so that there was no need of a new revelation to man, after Adam's creation to Noah, to give them the first idea or notion of the existence of a God; and not only of a God, but the true and living God. (44.)

We can see from this that Enos, Cainan, Mahalaleel, Jared, Methuselah, Lamech, and Noah, all lived on the earth at the same time; and that Enos, Cainan, Mahalaleel, Jared, Methuselah, and Lamech, were all acquainted with both Adam and Noah. (*Lectures on Faith* [Salt Lake City: N. B. Lundwall, compiler and publisher, no date], paragraph 43.)

Methuselah was the last of the antediluvian patriarchs to die, and he died in the 1656th year of the world's history (as per biblical chronology) which was the same year in which the flood came. (Second Lecture on Faith: 41.) Thus we see that for the first 1656 years of the world's history there was a sure knowledge of God among men.

The Prophet Joseph Smith tells us that Noah (as had Adam) held the keys of the priesthood and that holding the keys ". . . consisted in obtaining the voice of Jehovah that He talked with him [Noah] in a familiar and friendly manner, that He continued to him the keys, the covenants, the power and the glory, with which He blessed Adam at the beginning . . ." (*TPJS*:171.) Moses records: "And the Lord ordained Noah after his own order, and commanded him that he should go forth and declare his Gospel unto the children of men, even as it was given unto Enoch." (Moses 8:19.) Noah's message to his riotous generation was not merely personal and social morality (goodness) but he taught saying: "Believe and repent of your sins and be baptized in the name of Jesus Christ, the Son of God, even as our fathers, and ye shall receive the Holy Ghost, that ye may have all things made manifest; and if ye do not this, the floods will come in upon you; nevertheless they hearkened not." (*Ibid.*, 8:24.) However, ". . . Noah and his sons hearkened unto the Lord, and gave heed, and they were called the sons of God." (*Ibid.*, 8:13.) Noah, like Adam, had a sure knowledge of God and knew that salvation comes only through Jesus Christ, the Redeemer of the world.

Noah and his wife, their three sons, Shem, Ham, and Japheth, and their wives, survived the flood. In the ninth chapter of Genesis there is a strange story which reports that Noah began to be a husbandman and that he planted a vineyard, became drunken with wine, and that Ham saw Noah's nakedness, and that his nakedness was covered by his other sons. As a consequence when Noah awoke from his wine he pronounced a severe curse upon Ham and blessings upon Shem and Japheth. I personally believe there is much to this story which has not been preserved for us; however, what I wish to discuss at the moment is what Noah said to his sons when he awoke. The scripture reads:

> And he said, *Cursed be Canaan*; a servant of servants shall he be unto his brethren.
> And he said, Blessed be the *Lord God* of Shem; and Canaan shall be his servant.
> *God* shall enlarge Japheth, and he shall dwell in the tents of Shem; and Canaan shall be his servant. (Genesis 9:25-27. Italics mine.)

First, it is very interesting that although it was Ham who saw Noah's nakedness Noah did not say "Cursed be Ham," but he said, "Cursed be Canaan; a servant of servants shall he be unto his brethren." Canaan, of course, was Ham's son. As observed above, Ham was acknowledged as a son of God, and he was identified as one who walked with God, as did his father and his brothers. (Moses 8:27.) However, inasmuch as he married a Canaanite, his son Canaan was subject to the curse which was carried in the Canaanite line. Therefore, as pronounced by Noah, although it was Ham who reputedly saw Noah's nakedness, it was Canaan who was cursed.

The second thing we should note is that Noah said, "Blessed be the Lord God of Shem; and Canaan shall be his servant." It is of special interest here that in his reference to Shem, Noah used the name "Lord God," which refers to Jehovah. Of course, it was through Shem that the chosen lineage came, and it was they who were entrusted with the revelation of Jehovah, the pre-mortal Jesus.

On the contrary, when Noah spoke of the blessings to Japheth, he said: "God shall enlarge Japheth, and he shall dwell in the tents of Shem; and Canaan shall be his servant." Here he did not use the name for Jehovah the Redeemer, but he used the more generic name for God, Elohim. Japheth is the ancestor of the gentile nations and in Noah's pronouncement he used the name of Jehovah in relation to the covenant people, and he used the more generic name for the gentiles. He only pronounced a curse upon the descendants of Ham. The pronouncement upon Japheth in a way summarizes the whole. First, it suggests that Shem will be the possessor of the tents; Japheth is to be enlarged and be cared for by Shem; but Canaan will be the servant.

Chapter ten of Genesis gives us what is called the "Table of the Nations." Here we have a record of the immediate posterity of Shem, Ham, and Japheth and the parts of the world where they settled. With a proliferation of peoples came also a proliferation of religious opinions and beliefs.

One of the earliest and most influential apostates in the dispensation of Noah was named Nimrod, who was the son of Cush, who was the son of Ham. He was a mighty hunter and hero. He began a kingdom in Babel, Erech, and Accad (Shinar). Josephus tells us Nimrod excited the people to a contempt of God. He

persuaded the people to ascribe their well-being to himself instead of God. "He also changed the government
into tyranny, seeing no other way of turning man from
the fear of God, but to bring them into a constant dependence on his power." He also said ". . . he would
avenge himself on God for destroying their forefathers."
Furthermore, Josephus reports that Nimrod established his kingdom through rapine, murder, and tyranny. (Josephus, *Antiquities of the Jews*, Book I, chap.
4.) He urged the people to depart from the religion of
Shem and cleave to the institutes of Nimrod. (Clarke,
Bible Commentary, Vol. I, p. 84.) He tried to get men
to worship great conquerors and in time the deification
of humans became a chief characteristic of heathen religions in Egypt, Babylon, Greece, Rome, China, and
India. He also introduced animal worship. Idolatry
and adultery ("institutionalized immorality") became
common religious rites. Even human sacrifices were
instituted.

As nations of peoples came into being, the descendants of Japheth as well as those of Ham, they gradually
lost the gospel and substituted for it strange and perverse principles and practices. Even those who were
descended from Shem were not all faithful and in time
God gave a new dispensation to Abraham. Still later he
gave a new revelation to Moses. Eventually the Lord
Jesus Christ (Jehovah) himself came into the world.
He ministered on two hemispheres. After a short time
even the peoples he had visited apostatized. Indeed,
the story of man on the earth is one of his receiving the
gospel from heaven followed by an apostasy and in turn
followed by a restoration, etc.

Although the process of apostasies and restorations
with which we are generally most concerned are those
involving what we conventionally recognize as the
chosen lineage, there have been historical changes in

the beliefs and practices of peoples not of that lineage. Excluding the gospel, Hinduism is the oldest living world religion and is usually regarded as having its beginning in about 1500 B.C. Shintoism, Zoroastrianism, Taoism, Jainism, Buddhism, and Confucianism are generally dated from approximately 660 B.C. to 500 B.C. Muhammad, the founder of Islam, was reputedly born in 570 A.D. and Nanak, the founder of Sikhism, was reputedly born in 1469 A.D. Although one who believes in the gospel of Jesus Christ must look askance upon all of the other living world religions, he nonetheless must recognize some remarkable parallels (or at least analogous teachings) and that the establishment of those religions constituted a distinct moral advance for the peoples in the areas where they were established.

The estimated world population is three billion two hundred fifty million (3,250,000,000) persons. If the membership of The Church of Jesus Christ of Latter-day Saints is two million, one hundred thousand (2,100,000), the membership of the Church is only six hundredths of one per cent (.06) of the world population. At present the birth rate exceeds the death rate by approximately 150,000 persons every twenty-four hours. Consequently, the one hundred thousand (100,000) plus people we baptized last year was equivalent to the excess of births over deaths for only three-fourths of one day of the three hundred sixty-five days of the year. Although missionary work is greatly accelerated, and many would hope and pray that yet greater numbers of our Father's children will recognize the truth and hearken to it, it appears the simple truth is as the Doctrine and Covenants suggests, that the vast hordes of mankind will inherit the telestial kingdom of glory. (Section 76, verse 109.)

I have already suggested that the story of man on the earth is one of apostasies and restorations. The restorations have been due primarily to God's patience, long-suffering, forbearance, and love. The apostasies have been due to man's rebellious, perverse, recalcitrant, and proud disposition. As before suggested, although not mentioned, many people apostatized while Adam and the great patriarchs were still among them. The children of Israel worshipped a golden calf of their own making soon after being delivered by the Lord from a terrible bondage to the Egyptians. The majority of those who saw and heard the Lord among the Jews rejected him. Those who accepted him among the Nephites as well as among the Jews soon fell into apostasy. But apostasy on the earth was not an innovation for God's children, for a third of them apostatized in God's own presence while they were still spirit beings. It is little wonder that the masses of mankind are rebellious and have no proclivity for the gospel when we examine the record of rebelliousness of even those God has designated his chosen people.

Now, before considering some of the scriptures to see what they say regarding the world religions let us say just a word about the Latter-day Saint concept of man. In the first place the Lord has revealed that the original being which is called man was an intelligence. Furthermore, we are told that intelligences were not created by God but co-existed with him. In other words, whereas man as a spirit and man as a mortal is a contingent being, man as an intelligence is a necessary being. That is to say, his initial or original existence as an intelligence was not dependent upon God. However, in order that the intelligence could become a spirit and subsequently become a mortal was contingent upon certain conditions which involved dependence upon God. We assume that as independent entities, intelligences were free beings; at any rate when they were clothed with spirits as they were begotten by God as his Spirit offspring they were free agents. In the exercise of that agency all spirits did not make the same choices. Degrees of loyalty and devotion to God and the principles he taught his children ranged from those who were denominated "noble and great ones" to those who rebelled against him and were cast out of his presence. Factors in our development as spirits seem to have suggested to God the appropriate time and place for our mortal probation. For, as Paul said, God ". . . hath made of one blood all nations of men for to dwell on all the face of the earth, and hath determined the times before appointed, and the bounds of their habitation." (Acts 17: 22-26.) Moses had previously said: "When the Most High divided to the nations their inheritance, when he separated the sons of Adam, he set the bounds of the people according to the number of the children of Israel. For the Lord's portion is his people; Jacob is the lot of his inheritance." (Deuteronomy 32:8-9.) These statements by the prophets also suggest that God's spirit children would be born as mortals at times, in places, and environments, etc., in some way commensurate with their development in the pre-mortal spirit world. I believe we must assume that the statement in the Doctrine and Covenants that all blessings are predicated upon law and that ". . . when we obtain any blessing from God, it is by obedience to that law upon which it is predicated" (D&C 130:21), obtains with reference to the pre-mortal spirit world and coming into this world as well as while we are in this world, and when we enter the post-mortal spirit world and resurrected state. However, I also believe there are complex factors involved and that we must avoid the hasty and perhaps unwarranted and erroneous assumption that circumstances in this world which from a mortal perspective would normally be considered most favorable, less favorable, and least favorable necessarily mean that every individual who comes into those circumstances was necessarily most valiant, less valiant, and least valiant in the spirit world among those who will be permitted to become souls, or acquire physical bodies.

Irrespective of the complexities involved here it is a fact that the Lord has restored his gospel to the earth and that there are also many religions and sects within religions now among men. Ignoring the primitive or tribal religions and only considering the so-called world religions, or possibly "higher" religions, it is interesting to observe that they have something of a common denominator in a principle which variously approximates the second of the two great commandments. With the diminishing regard of Jesus Christ as divine and as literally the Son of God, the Redeemer of the world, etc., by some so-called Christians in our century, and the growing tendency to regard him as a great moral teacher only, perhaps the greatest, has naturally led to a more compatible theological relationship between what the world calls Christianity and the other world religions. In effect, theology bows out to morality, thinking of theology as the science or study of God and morality as the science or study of human conduct. Too often theology is now considered a sterile enterprise either on the grounds that God does not exist and man has no future beyond mortality, or on the grounds that if God does exist, all is relative anyway and all that really matters is human conduct—man's relation with man. The truth of the matter seems to be that the theology which is known to the world in general *is* a sterile enterprise, but because mankind in general is in an apostate condition, the truth perverted, and the light of revelation lost among them, rather than *on* the grounds they assume.

Let us consider a few passages of scripture given to the world in this dispensation and see what they say which relates to the so-called world religions. Here are some of the things Nephi recorded:

Know ye not that there are more nations than one? Know ye not that I, the Lord your God, have created all men, and that I remember those who are upon the isles of the sea; and that I rule in the heavens above and in the earth beneath; and I bring forth my word unto the children of men, yea, even upon all the nations of the earth?

Wherefore murmur ye, because that ye shall receive more of my word? Know ye not that the testimony of two nations is a witness unto you that I am God, that I remember one nation like unto another? Wherefore, I speak the same words unto one nation like unto another. And when the two nations shall run together the testimony of the two nations shall run together also.

And I do this that I may prove unto many that I am the same yesterday, today, and forever; and that I speak forth my words according to mine own pleasure. And because that I have spoken one word ye need not suppose that I cannot speak another; for my work is not yet finished; neither shall it be until the end of man, neither from that time henceforth and forever.

Wherefore, because that ye have a Bible ye need not suppose that it contains all my words; neither need ye suppose that I have not caused more to be written.

For I command all men, both in the east and in the west, and in the north, and in the south, and in the islands of the sea, that they shall write the words which I speak unto them; for out of the books which shall be written I will judge the world, every man according to their works, according to that which is written.

For behold, I shall speak unto the Jews and they shall write it; and I shall also speak unto the Nephites and they shall write it; and I shall also speak unto the other tribes of the house of Israel, which I have led away, and they shall write it; and I shall also speak unto all nations of the earth and they shall write it.

And it shall come to pass that the Jews shall have the words of the Nephites, and the Nephites shall have the words of the Jews; and the Nephites and the Jews shall have the words of the lost tribes of Israel; and the lost tribes of Israel shall have the words of the Nephites and the Jews.

And it shall come to pass that my people, which are of the house of Israel, shall be gathered home unto the lands of their possessions; and my word also shall be gathered in one. And I will show unto them that fight against my word and against my people, who are of the house of Israel, that I am God, and that I covenanted with Abraham that I would remember his seed forever. (2 Nephi 29:7-14.)

There are many ideas in these verses upon which one is tempted to ponder, but here I merely wish to enumerate several points from these verses:

1. God created all men.
2. God brings forth his word unto men upon all the nations of the earth.
3. God commands men everywhere to write the words he speaks unto them.
4. God shall speak unto all nations of the earth, and they shall write it.
5. Out of the books men will be judged.
6. God is to speak to the Jews, Nephites, and other tribes of the house of Israel, and they shall have their records in common.
7. God's people are the house of Israel, and his word shall be gathered in one.

King Benjamin declared:

For behold, and also his blood atoneth for the sins of those who have fallen by the transgression of Adam, who have died not knowing the will of God concerning them, or who have ignorantly sinned.

But wo, wo unto him who knoweth that he rebelleth against God! For salvation cometh to none such except it be through repentance and faith on the Lord Jesus Christ.

And the Lord God hath sent his holy prophets among all the children of men, to declare these things to every kindred, nation, and tongue, that thereby whosoever should believe that Christ should come, the same might receive remission of their sins, and rejoice with exceeding great joy, even as though he had already come among them.

Yet the Lord God saw that his people were a stiffnecked people, and he appointed unto them a law, even the law of Moses.

And many signs, and wonders, and types, and shadows showed he unto them, concerning his coming; and also holy prophets spake unto them concerning his coming; and yet they hardened their hearts, and understood not that the law of Moses availeth nothing except it were through the atonement of his blood. (Mosiah 3:11-15.)

Again, let us enumerate only a few points:

1. Salvation comes only through the atonement of Jesus' blood.
2. Salvation is only for those who repent and have faith on the Lord Jesus Christ.
3. God has sent his holy prophets among all the children of men to declare Christ.

Our record is incomplete regarding the declaration of the gospel to every kindred, nation, and tongue, but the revelations are clear that all men will have the opportunity of accepting or rejecting it prior to their final judgment.

Alma gives us this significant insight:

For behold, the Lord doth grant unto all nations, of their own nation and tongue, to teach his word, yea, in wisdom all that he seeth fit that they should have; therefore we see that the Lord doth counsel in wisdom, according to that which is just and true. (Alma 29:8.)

There are two points here I wish to emphasize:

1. God grants all nations prophets of their own to teach his word.
2. God grants all nations all that in his wisdom he seeth fit that they should have.

In another place Alma gives us these very helpful words:

It is given unto many to know the mysteries of God; nevertheless they are laid under a strict command that they

shall not impart only according to the portion of his word
which he doth grant unto the children of men, according to the
heed and diligence which they give unto him.

And therefore, he that will harden his heart, the same receiveth the lesser portion of the word; and he that will
not harden his heart, to him is given the greater portion of the
word, until it is given unto him to know the mysteries of God
until he know them in full.

And they that will harden their hearts, to them is given
the lesser portion of the word until they know nothing concerning his mysteries; and then they are taken captive by the devil,
and led by his will down to destruction. Now this is what is
meant by the chains of hell. (*Ibid.*, 12:9-11.)

Let us note these points particularly:

1. God's word is granted according to man's heed
   and diligence.
2. The hardhearted are given the lesser portion of
   the word.
3. To those who are not hardhearted is given the
   greater portion.
4. The hardhearted receive less and less until they
   are lost.

I believe the Lord gave us an illustration of the general principle which is involved here through Mormon.
Some readers will recall that Mormon records the following, speaking of our Book of Mormon:

And when they shall have received this, which is expedient
that they should have first, to try their faith, and if it shall so
be that they shall believe these things then shall the greater
things be made manifest unto them.

And if it so be that they will not believe these things, then
shall the greater things be withheld from them, unto their condemnation. (3 Nephi 26:9-10.)

I would summarize the foregoing briefly by saying
God created all men, that he grants all nations prophets
of their own to teach his word, that men are commanded
to write the words he speaks to them, that if they are

hardhearted they receive a lesser portion, and if they are not hardhearted they receive a greater portion, that salvation comes only to those who repent and have faith in Jesus Christ and his atonement, and finally God grants to nations all that in his wisdom he seeth fit that they should have, and that according to their heed and diligence.

There are eleven living world religions and a host of churches, sects, and cults, and yet the angel of the Lord told Nephi the son of Lehi that there are only two churches. He said:

Behold there are save two churches only; the one is the church of the Lamb of God, and the other is the church of the devil; wherefore, whoso belongeth not to the church of the Lamb of God belongeth to that great church, which is the mother of abominations; and she is the whore of all the earth. (1 Nephi 14:10.)

Nephi comments:

And it came to pass that I looked and beheld the whore of all the earth, and she sat upon many waters; and she had dominion over all the earth, among all nations, kindreds, tongues, and people.

And it came to pass that I beheld the church of the Lamb of God, and its numbers were few, because of the wickedness and abominations of the whore who sat upon many waters; nevertheless, I beheld that the church of the Lamb, who were the saints of God, were also upon all the face of the earth; and their dominions upon the face of the earth were small, because of the wickedness of the great whore whom I saw. (*Ibid.*, 14: 11-12.)

There are only two churches, the church of the Lamb of God whose numbers are few, and the church of the devil whose numbers have dominion over all nations, etc.

Now, just what is meant by the two churches when we apply that concept to all of the nominally religious institutions, formal and informal, which are found on the earth?

I am sure that there are some who would choose to interpret this in what I have chosen to call the humanistic sense. According to that interpretation the church of the Lamb of God would be identified as all of those persons who are striving to promote goodness in the moral sense—personal and social—irrespective of institutional affiliation, etc. Similarly the church of the devil would be those who fail to promote goodness and those who promote evil.

The other interpretation is what I have chosen to call the legal one. According to that interpretation the church of the Lamb of God is that institution established by the Lord which through him possesses the power to make its adherents become heirs to the celestial kingdom. Correspondingly the church of the devil consists of those institutions which purportedly have within them the power of salvation but which in truth lack the power to make their adherents heirs of the celestial kingdom. Simply put, the gospel of Jesus Christ is designed to change the lives of men through the redemption of Christ so they can enter the celestial kingdom. Any institution which has not the power to open the door of that kingdom falls short of being the church of the Lamb of God and therefore constitutes a part of the church of the devil. This means in effect, that apostate Christianity and all of the world religions with their various cults and sects constitute parts of the church of the devil. God wants his children to heed his word and develop themselves so they love the law and adhere to the law and can enter his presence as celestial beings. Lucifer wants to thwart the work of God and strives to keep men and women from achieving the celestial kingdom.

It should be pointed out here that when the Prophet Joseph Smith and Sidney Rigdon were given the vision of the three degrees of glory they were shown that those who reject the gospel as mortals but receive it afterwards, the honorable men of the earth, and those who are not valiant in the testimony of Jesus, will inherit the terrestrial kingdom. (D&C 76:71-80.)

Also, they wrote the following with regard to the telestial kingdom:

> For these are they who are of Paul, and of Apollos, and of Cephas.
>
> These are they who say they are some of one and some of another—some of Christ and some of John, and some of Moses, and some of Elias, and some of Esaias, and some of Isaiah, and some Enoch;
>
> But received not the gospel, neither the testimony of Jesus, neither the prophets, *neither the everlasting covenant.* (*Ibid.,* 76:99-101. Italics mine.)

It is likely that if one should oppose this interpretation and prefer what I have called the humanistic interpretation or some modification of it, he would offer in his defense a passage from Alma. It reads:

> For I say unto you that whatsoever is good cometh from God, and whatsoever is evil cometh from the devil. (Alma 5: 40.)

This is the type verse which is so often lifted out of its context and when used in isolation is either wittingly or unwittingly given a different meaning from that of its context. Here is the verse in its context:

> Behold, I say unto you, that the good shepherd doth call you; yea, and in his own name he doth call you, which is the name of Christ; and if ye will not hearken unto the voice of the good shepherd, to the name by which ye are called, behold, ye are not the sheep of the good shepherd.
>
> And now if ye are not the sheep of the good shepherd, of what fold are ye? Behold, I say unto you, that the devil is your shepherd, and ye are of his fold; and now, who can deny this?

Behold, I say unto you, whosoever denieth this is a liar and a child of the devil.

For I say unto you that whatsoever is good cometh from God, and whatsoever is evil cometh from the devil.

Therefore, if a man bringeth forth good works he hearkeneth unto the voice of the good shepherd, and he doth follow him; but whosoever bringeth forth evil works, the same becometh a child of the devil, for he hearkeneth unto his voice, and doth follow him. (*Ibid.*, 5:38-41.)

The first thing one should observe here is that good is identified with hearkening unto the voice of the good Shepherd and recognizing that he calls in his own name which is the name of Christ. Second, it should be observed that either one is of the fold of Christ or he is of the fold of the devil. (Please keep in mind that the principles and ordinances of the restored gospel are not requirements for entrance into the telestial glory or the terrestrial glory, but for the celestial glory.) The third thing we should observe in Alma's passage is that he is distinguishing between good and evil, not good and bad. This is a technical distinction, but I believe it is a very important one. The contrast between good and bad is generally thought of as describing human values, or perhaps it would be better to say values viewed from a human or temporal perspective. This would be applicable if the humanistic interpretation of the two-church passage were the correct one. On the contrary, the contrast between good and evil is generally thought of as describing values as viewed from a divine or eternal perspective. This is applicable in the legal interpretation of the two-church passage. Another way of trying to make the point that is involved here is to say that personal and social morality are not all that are required of one to be a member of the church of the Lamb of God and enter the celestial kingdom. Surely one must keep those commandments which have to do with human conduct (or morality in the generic sense), but he must also be willing to take upon himself the name of Christ and do all of those things which are appropriate to the privilege of bearing that sacred name.

In a revelation to the Prophet Joseph Smith the Lord said the following, which has bearing on this point:

For whoso cometh not unto me is under the bondage of sin.

And whoso receiveth not my voice is not acquainted with my voice, and is not of me.

And *by this you may know the righteous from the wicked,* and that the whole world groaneth under sin and darkness even now. (D&C 84: 51-53. Italics mine.)

Let me illustrate further from the Sermon on the Mount. In the King James version we find the following:

Blessed are they which are persecuted for righteousness' sake: for theirs is the kingdom of heaven. (Matthew 5:10.)

This suggests the promises are conditioned upon the defense of goodness, righteousness. Certainly I do not want to minimize the necessity of goodness, but I believe that what the Lord said when he gave the same sermon to the Nephites indicates that he was speaking of something more comprehensive and inclusive than goodness or righteousness in conduct alone. To the Nephites he said:

And blessed are all they who are persecuted for my name's sake, for theirs is the kingdom of heaven. (3 Nephi 12:10.)

Men and women must be willing not only to stand firm in the defense of and be persecuted if necessary for righteousness or goodness, but they must be willing to bear his name (Jesus' name) valiantly.

I hope it is not assumed from the foregoing that it is the intent of this chapter that we must conclude that all persons outside The Church of Jesus Christ of Latter-day Saints are evil. We must distinguish between the institutions which constitute the church of the devil and the individuals who have not yet made covenants with the Lord at the hands of his authorized servants. I believe we must recognize the religions of the world (excluding the gospel) as substitutes for the gospel. No doubt many good or righteous men have been raised up among the peoples of the earth and have striven to obtain as much light and truth as they could. No doubt some of these men have been rewarded for their earnestness and have been blessed by the Holy Spirit. That is, they have been given the gospel through the power of the Holy Ghost, but through the Holy Spirit which is available to all men they have been given that which was appropriate for them and for their contemporaries. They were given principles according to their heed and diligence as the Lord in his wisdom saw fit. This view does not contradict the fact that they still belong to the church of the devil for although they have been blessed to receive light through the Holy Spirit which has helped them to improve themselves and others, they still lack certain principles and the ordinances, which are necessary to enter the church of the Lamb of God.

To some this may seem harsh. But we must recall that on one occasion when the Lord was explaining certain doctrines, many of his disciples said: "This is an hard saying." But the fact that it was thought to be a hard saying in no way altered the truth of the matter.

When the Lord spoke to Joseph Smith in the first vision he spoke plainly with regard to the sects of the day. The Prophet reports:

I was answered that I must join none of them, for they were all wrong; and the Personage who addressed me said that all their creeds were an abomination in his sight. . . . (Joseph Smith 2:19.)

We should also remember that the Lord declared to Nephi that men should write the words which he would speak unto them and that out of the books which would be written he will judge the world, "every man according to their works, according to that which is written." (2 Nephi 29:11.)

But we must not lose sight of the fact that there is a chosen people by covenant. The Lord said to Abraham:

My name is Jehovah, and I know the end from the beginning; therefore my hand shall be over thee.

And I will make of thee a great nation, and I will bless thee above measure, and make thy name great among all nations, and thou shalt be a blessing unto thy seed after thee, that in their hands they shall bear this ministry and Priesthood unto all nations;

And I will bless them through thy name; for as many as receive this Gospel shall be called after thy name, and shall be accounted thy seed, and shall rise up and bless thee, as their father;

And I will bless them that bless thee, and curse them that curse thee; and in thee (that is, in thy Priesthood) and in thy seed (that is, thy Priesthood), for I give unto thee a promise that this right shall continue in thee, and in thy seed after thee (that is to say, the literal seed or the seed of the body) shall all the families of the earth be blessed, even with the blessings of the Gospel, which are the blessings of salvation, even of life eternal. (Abraham 2:8-11.)

These great verses are significant not only because they clearly point up the patriarchal covenant which Jehovah made with Abraham and his seed, and the priesthood nature of that covenant, but because they also clearly indicate that as many as will take the covenant upon themselves, be they literal descendants and natural heirs of the house of Israel or not, if they will receive the gospel shall be called after Abraham's name, be accounted his seed, and shall receive all of the blessings of the covenant. Being born outside the natural lineage of Abraham does not preclude one's obtaining the blessings of the covenant through faithfulness any more than being born within the natural covenant of Israel is an irrevocable guarantee that one will receive the blessings of that covenant. As Nephi said:

For behold, I say unto you that as many of the Gentiles as will repent are the covenant people of the Lord; and as many of the Jews as will not repent shall be cast off; for the Lord covenanteth with none save it be with them that repent and believe in his Son, who is the Holy One of Israel. (2 Nephi 30:2.)

Also, the word of the Lord to Nephi was:

. . . I will give unto the children of men line upon line, precept upon precept, here a little and there a little; and blessed are those who hearken unto my precepts, and lend an ear unto my counsel, for they shall learn wisdom; for unto him that receiveth I will give more; and from them that shall say, We have enough, from them shall be taken away even that which they have.

Cursed is he that putteth his trust in man, or maketh flesh his arm, or shall hearken unto the precepts of men, save their precepts shall be given by the power of the Holy Ghost. (*Ibid.*, 28:30-31.)

We live in the Dispensation of the Fulness of Times, and with the wonderful physical blessings which have come to the world in our time there are greater facilities for giving all mankind an opportunity to hear the gospel than the world has ever known. As the Prophet Joseph Smith declared:

We claim the privilege of worshiping Almighty God according to the dictates of our own conscience, and allow all men the same privilege, let them worship how, where, or what they may,

but we must distinguish between tolerance, indifference, and acceptance. (See 11th Article of Faith.)

Men are free to worship as they please, but the price or blessing of that freedom is that they must accept the consequences of their choice.

The Lord has given the following charge to the Latter-day Saints:

Hearken, O ye people of my church, saith the voice of him who dwells on high, and whose eyes are upon all men;

yea, verily I say: Hearken ye people from afar; and ye that are upon the islands of the sea, listen together.

For verily the voice of the Lord is unto all men, and there is none to escape; and there is no eye that shall not see, neither ear that shall not hear, neither heart that shall not be penetrated.

And the rebellious shall be pierced with much sorrow; for their iniquities shall be spoken upon the housetops, and their secret acts shall be revealed.

And the voice of warning shall be unto all people, by the mouths of my disciples, whom I have chosen in these last days.

And they shall go forth and none shall stay them, for I the Lord have commanded them.

Behold, this is mine authority, and the authority of my servants, and my preface unto the book of my commandments, which I have given them to publish unto you, O inhabitants of the earth.

Wherefore, fear and tremble, O ye people, for what I the Lord have decreed in them shall be fulfilled.

* * *

What I the Lord have spoken, I have spoken, and I excuse not myself; and though the heavens and the earth pass away, my word shall not pass away, but shall all be fulfilled, whether by mine own voice or by the voice of my servants, it is the same. (D&C 1:1-7, 38.)

The Church of Jesus Christ of Latter-day Saints declares to the world that salvation comes only through Jesus and his restored gospel. As King Benjamin said:

. . . there shall be no other name given nor any other way nor means whereby salvation can come unto the children of men, only in and through the name of Christ, the Lord Omnipotent.

For behold he judgeth, and his judgment is just; and the infant perisheth not that dieth in his infancy; but men drink damnation to their own souls except they humble themselves and become as little children, and believe that salvation was, and is, and is to come, in and through the atoning blood of Christ, the Lord Omnipotent. (Mosiah 3:17-18.)

There is only one true gospel, and as President Brigham Young proclaimed in unmistakable language:

The gospel which we preach is the gospel of life and salvation. The Church which we represent is the Church and
Kingdom of God, and possesses the only faith by which
the children of men can be brought back into the presence of
our Father and God. The Lord has set his hands to restore all
things as in the beginning, and by the administration of His
Holy Priesthood, save all who can be saved, cleanse from the
world the consequences of the fall and give it to the hands of
His Saints. (*JD* 12:205 or *DBY*: 4.)

Furthermore, he said:

. . . we have something more than morality alone to teach
the people. What is it? It is how to redeem the human family.
(*JD* 19:47 or *DBY*: 5.)

I will now say to my friends—and I call you all, and all
mankind, friends, until you have proved yourselves enemies,—
you who do not belong to this Church, that we have got the gospel of life and salvation. I do not say that we have *a* gospel,
but I say that we have *the* definite and only gospel that ever
was or ever will be that will save the children of men. (*JD* 12:
313 or *DBY*:5. Italics mine.)

And he also said:

We declare it to all the inhabitants of the earth from the
valleys in the tops of these mountains that we are The Church
of Jesus Christ of Latter-day Saints—not a church but the
Church—and we have the doctrine of life and salvation for all
the honest-in-heart in all the world. (*JD* 12:173 or *DBY*: 7.)

As recorded by John, the Lord himself announced:

I am the way, the truth, and the life: no man cometh unto
the Father, but by me. (John 14:6.)

In order that there may be no mistaking the fact
that it is through him and him alone that one can be
forgiven of his sins, the Lord said:

. . . for if ye believe not that I am he, ye shall die in your
sins. (*Ibid.*, 8:24.)

The central place of the Lord Jesus Christ is made
very emphatic when he declared "he that receiveth me

receiveth him that sent me" (*ibid.*, 13:20) but perhaps the strongest statement attributed to the Lord is where he said "He that hateth me hateth my Father also." (*Ibid.*, 15:23.) Inasmuch as God is the God and Father of all, this seems to suggest in no uncertain terms that those who talk about believing in God and loving God and things of that kind but who reject the Christ know not whereof they speak and can only mean that their belief and love is centered only in some creature of their own imagination and hopes.

All of the foregoing should cause a Latter-day Saint to realize in some measure what a tremendously grave responsibility rests upon him as one of the infinitesimally small number of God's children upon the earth who have made covenants with him. In the partial realization of the remarkable blessings which are his, he must not permit himself to fall into the trap of pride. He must strive to be humble in all that he does from day to day and continuously seek the incomparable companionship of the Holy Ghost. He must remember that God is the Father of all men. All men are brothers. God loves all of his children. The gospel is a message to all of God's children, and each man and woman will be blessed to the extent that he or she strives to do the Lord's will, and every man will ultimately receive all that he will receive. (See D&C 88:32.)

As individuals, blessed as are the Latter-day Saints, they must manifest an attitude of love, compassion, patience, and understanding toward all who do not know the truth and strive in the spirit of those attributes to teach them the gospel by precept and example. In the words of the prophets, the Saints must be "nursing fathers" and "nursing mothers" to them.

Chapter XIII

GOD AS CREATOR AND MAN AS CREATOR

When we speak of God as Creator, what do we mean? John the Apostle, in the first chapter of his gospel, speaking of the "Word" that was in the beginning with God and was also God, says: "All things were made by him; and without him was not anything made that was made." (John 1:1-3.)

Similarly, Paul, in writing of God to the Hebrews, said: he "hath in these last days spoken unto us by his Son, whom he hath appointed heir of all things, by whom also he made the worlds." (Hebrews 1:2.)

In our own dispensation Joseph Smith and Sidney Rigdon were given a glorious vision in which they heard a voice bearing record of the Son, Jesus Christ, saying: "That by him, and through him, and of him, the worlds are and were created, and the inhabitants thereof are begotten sons and daughters unto God." (D&C 76:24.)

In a great ancient vision given to Moses he beheld the earth, all the inhabitants thereof, and also "beheld many lands," each of which was called earth and saw their inhabitants. (Moses 1:29.)

Moses said to God: "Tell me, I pray thee, why these things are so, and by what thou madest them?" Then as Moses talked with God face to face, the Lord said unto him: "For mine own purpose have I made these things. Here is wisdom and it remaineth in me.

"And by the word of my power, have I created them, which is mine Only Begotten Son, who is full of grace and truth.

"And worlds without number have I created; and I also created them for mine own purpose; and by the Son I created them, which is mine Only Begotten." (See *ibid.*, 1:27-33.)

Further, the Lord continued to Moses by telling him many worlds have passed away by the word of his power and many now stand and that although they are innumerable unto man they are numbered unto him (God). (*Ibid.*, 1:35-38.)

Among the things we learn from these passages which we should note here are the following:

1. John declares all things were made by the Word, *i.e.*, by Jehovah, the pre-mortal Jesus.
2. Paul affirms Jesus Christ as appointed heir of all things and that it was by him that God made the worlds.
3. By a modern vision and heavenly declaration Joseph Smith and Sidney Rigdon witness that it was "by," "through," and "of" Jesus Christ that the worlds are and were created.
4. Moses was shown this earth, its inhabitants, and many lands called earth and that they had inhabitants.
5. The Lord said the worlds and their inhabitants are innumerable unto man though they are numbered unto him.
6. God told Moses he had created the worlds.
7. He said he created them by the Son, his Only Begotten.
8. He also told Moses the creation was for his own purpose.

In another verse in this same passage the Lord revealed the purpose of creation unto Moses when he said: "For behold, this is my work and my glory—to bring to pass the immortality and eternal life of man." (*Ibid.*, 1:39.)

It seems, therefore, when we speak of God as creator, we are suggesting a causal relation between God, and the worlds and their inhabitants, in which God is cause and the worlds and their inhabitants are effects.

Though this is the case, it should not be assumed God is the Absolute or Sole Cause.

As is well-known, the Prophet Joseph Smith said "... the word create came from the word *baurau*, which does not mean to create out of nothing; it means to organize; the same as a man would organize materials and build a ship." (*TPJS*: 350.)

Here "create" does not mean bring into being in the sense of bringing into existence from total non-existence, but on the contrary it means bring into being in the sense of to form, organize, reorganize, or structure that which already exists in a state of chaos, or in some other elementary condition.

The Lord has either revealed, or from his revelations it can be reasonably inferred, that all of the following are eternal, that is, have always existed:

1. Element (matter)
2. Intelligences
3. Time
4. Space
5. Kingdoms
6. Laws

At present we can only concern ourselves with the first two, element and intelligences.

In a very profound revelation given to Joseph Smith in May of 1833 the Lord declared: "The elements are eternal. . . ." (D&C 93:33.)

The Prophet Joseph Smith, in a discourse, said, "Element had an existence from the time he [God] had. The pure principles of element are principles which can never be destroyed; they may be organized and reorganized, but not destroyed. They had no beginning, and can have no end." (*TPJS*:351-352.)

That which we think of as the common stuff out of which the things of the world are made is eternal. We experience the natural things called the soil, rocks, hills, mountains, streams, rivers, lakes, and oceans, with numberless hosts of vegetable, insect, and animal life upon or in them, and we are given to understand the physical stuff which constitutes these sensible realities is eternal. God is their Creator in the sense that he is responsible for their having been organized, but they were organized from eternally existing elements and according to eternal law.

The Lord has also revealed that the original "you," or the original "me" is an entity called an intelligence. In one place he says: "Man was also in the beginning with God. Intelligence, or the light of truth, was not created or made, neither indeed can be." (D&C 93:29.)

The Prophet Joseph Smith declared God is a self-existent being and that man exists upon the same principle. (*TPJS*:352.) Further, he said: "The intelligence of spirits had no beginning, neither will it have an end." (*Ibid.*:353.) "Intelligence is eternal and exists upon a self-existent principle. It is a spirit [entity, individual] from age to age, and there is no creation about it." (*Ibid.*:354.)

Essentially the revelations and the Prophet Joseph Smith declare that the original beings, which in our present estate we speak of as mortals, are uncreated. The intelligences, or the original entities, were not formed, organized, structured, made, created, nor begotten of God. They have co-existed with God from eternity.

Although God provided bodies of spirit for the intelligences, and provided this earthly abode for them, as well as the means for them to come here, along with a program for their individual development and progression, he did not originate, create, nor bring them into being or existence.

The creature we call man, therefore, consists of three fundamental realities: intelligence, spirit, and body. The body consists of physical element which is eternal but is produced or formed through the process of mortal begetting. The spirit also, according to revelation, consists of physical element, which is more fine and pure than that of ordinary mortal experience, and is also eternal; but the spirit is produced or formed through a process of divine or celestial begetting or procreation. On the contrary, the intelligence is not begotten but is that entity which is clothed with a body of spirit by celestial parents.

Man as mortal is therefore a contingent being. Man as spirit is likewise a contingent being. But man as intelligence is a necessary being.

Mortals should take no special pride in the necessity of their original being, however, for they share this characteristic in common with all other things which exist. Furthermore, they would have remained in that original state were it not for God's goodness in having provided spirit bodies, the light of eternal truth, and opportunities for progression.

From the foregoing it is apparent that God is man's Creator, but not in the sense of having brought him into being out of non-existence, but in the sense of having begotten him—having provided the eternally existing intelligence with a tabernacle of spirit.

The revelations declare God is the Creator of heaven and earth and all things that in them are. The world and its embellishments are the handiwork of God through eternally organizing processes; however, man is his son. The worlds are God's domain. Mankind is his family.

When we look at the world, using the word "world" here to mean the animate and inanimate physical environment in which mortals live, we find that creative processes, in the sense of organizing, forming, producing, etc., manifest themselves on a continuum of levels of complexity.

In a modern revelation the Lord said, in speaking of the kingdoms of man's eternal habitation:

All kingdoms have a law given;
And there are many kingdoms; for there is no space in the which there is no kingdom; and there is no kingdom in which there is no space, either a greater or a lesser kingdom.
And unto every kingdom is given a law; and unto every law there are certain bounds also and conditions." (D&C 88: 36-38.)

The context of the passage seems to indicate the Lord was speaking explicitly regarding the macrocosm; however, man's limited finite experience suggests that the same principle obtains for each microcosm.

The following is an interesting example which illustrates the complexity and creativity which is characteristic of the cosmic arena in which we live.

The fig tree, to take a third example, bears a complex flower, actually a collection of small flowers within the synconium or receptacle. The orifice of this receptacle is very small. The flowers almost fill the entire cavity. The female flower consists of a pistil and ovary, containing a single ovule. Some kinds of figs have two different forms of female flowers in the same synconium—some with short styles (the terminals of the ovaries) and short stigmas (the part of the pistil that receives the pollen). These latter are called gallflowers because they are produced for the use and convenience of the gall wasp, a very small insect. The gallflowers are, as a rule, placed low in the synconium, and the male flowers, which consist of only a single stamen, are near the mouth.

The gall wasp enters the fig by the orifice, crawls down until it reaches the gallflowers and sinks its ovipositor, a specialized organ for depositing its eggs, down the style canal. It then lays an egg close to the nucleus of the ovule. Later the larva of the wasp feeds on the substance of the ovule, which is sufficient for its development.

The male wasps emerge from the ovules earlier than the females. Beings wingless, they do not leave the synconium, but visit the gallflowers, containing female wasps, and fertilize them. When the fertilized females emerge, they crawl up the synconium and become dusted with pollen from the male flowers. When their wings have expanded and dried, they seek out other fig flowers which are at an earlier stage of development. They lay their eggs in the ovaries, being careful to select only the gallflowers with undeveloped stigmas—which seem to have been specially developed for them.

The true female flowers with long styles are, however, also dusted by the pollen. Should the wasp make a mistake— which is doubtful—and lay an egg in a true female flower, the egg will not develop, because the style is too long for the wasp's ovipositor to reach the ovule upon which the larva feeds. In short, the egg is left in an unfavorable place. The gallflowers with short styles and stigmas, on the other hand, are well adapted to receive the egg and seem to have been specially provided by the fig for the wasp's convenience. In return for this service, the wasp carries the pollen from one flower to another. (See E. L. Grant Watson's, "The Hidden Heart of Nature," *Saturday Evening Post* for May 27, 1961, pp. 91-92.)

There may be some persons who would protest by saying there is no creativity involved in that illustration. The growth of the tree with its flowers and the laying of the eggs of the wasp, etc., are at most natural and instinctive processes, respectively. In my opinion, the fact that the processes described are natural and instinctive in no way means that they are not also creative. In fact, each, in contributing to the fulfillment of the other, concomitantly contributes to the development of itself.

But, some of those persons may say, "real" creativity belongs only to man—the rational animal. To which, I respond, Yes, man is a rational being, and should be *grateful* for rather than *proud* of his rationality, and *should* be *humbled* by the tremendous blessing and responsibility of this endowment.

But, I must ask, "What do you mean by 'real' creativity?" To which a multitude of answers may take the general form of, "The creation of the artist, the musician, the sculptor, the writer, the inventor, the research scientist," etc.

This has a familiar ring to it and seems to be obvious. However, upon inquiry I wonder if even the remarkable contributions of persons of the types enumerated can qualify as examples of "real" creativity.

First of all, although the so-called creative one is a rational being, as compared to the tree and the wasp, is he not essentially, like them, engaged in a process of fulfilling or realizing his own capacities or potentialities as he gives of himself in his own enterprises?

We speak of the processes such as those manifest in the growth and development of trees as natural, and those of insects and animals as instinctive, and those of man as rational, progressively rising on the ontological ladder. However, in the larger sense of the word, are not all of these kinds of things engaged in kinds of processes which are natural to them and consistent with the word of the Lord that there is no space without a kingdom and that unto every kingdom a law is given.

Obviously, if we think of man as a species, his creativeness is manifest in a multitude of ways as compared with the rigorous limitations in other species.

Second, although the so-called creative one is a rational being, as compared to the tree and the wasp, and creates new art pieces, invents new devices, or makes great discoveries, his creative acts can hardly mean "real" creativity if by "real" we mean original, for as great as the particular contribution may be, it is not original, for it was *found* in the encyclopedia of the universe.

The laws and principles of all things are eternal, and man through his ardent searchings and other creative skills is able from time to time to penetrate some secret corner of some page of that vast eternal volume. But, as the Apostle Paul said in another context, ". . . now we see through a glass, darkly." (1 Cor. 13:12.)

Just as God did not create element and intelligences *ex nihilo,* or out of, or from nothing, but organized them according to eternally existing laws and principles, so man should not be grieved to be told that he is not "really" the originator or discoverer or creator in any *ex nihilo* sense, but only in some secondary sense of being an organizer, a former, a structurer.

Creativity, in this sense of the word, has revealed itself among men in a host of ways. It manifests itself in the fine arts, the pure sciences, the applied arts, applied sciences, the humanities, the social sciences, the medical arts, etc. Creativity may be primarily a product of the mind, it may be also a product of manual dexterity, or it may require skills in human relations. Too often the word "creativity" is conceived so narrowly that it precludes all but a few limited skills or abilities. But this kind of narrowness implies an inherent exclusiveness which is a source of great satisfaction to some egos.

However, it is my opinion that life itself is a creative process. And that far more important than any particular single creative achievement which might be heralded in the world is the creative process which occurs in the individual human being, not as a so-called great event for the world, but as the fulfillment of self, or development of one's capacities, or realization of one's potentialities. Creativity in the fullest sense of the word, as I conceive it, has to do not with the creation of things but with the fulfillment of self.

The revealed gospel of our Lord emphasizes the point that it has been given to mankind that he might *become* God's sons and daughters in very deed in addition to being his spiritual offspring. *Being* his spirit offspring is not enough to be like him. We must *become* like him, and that is a process. Therefore, if man's creative interests and efforts are merely or primarily absorbed in the things being created rather than in what is happening to human beings, his creativity has gone awry.

Why should man be a creator or be creative? Summarily, because it is his nature and his destiny.

We have already stressed the point that all of creation, so to speak, is creative.

The magnitude of the vast complex of creative forces in the world is so multitudinous that it is almost overwhelming to try to contemplate it.

And inasmuch as man is not merely a thing nor an "it," but belongs to the race of God, as his offspring, he is more greatly endowed with creative capacities than things.

Furthermore, the Lord has revealed that his children who are most responsive to the most important eternal principles will be most richly blessed thereby and will discover the effect of divine-creative forces within them as mortals and will eventually realize their ultimate destiny in becoming not only blessed sons and daughters of God, but they shall pass by the angels and even become gods. (See D&C 132.)

From that great perspective, surely some of man's mortally regarded great creations must appear as simple as the small infant's fumbling effort to say "da-da," or "ma-ma."

Be humble, O man, and glory not in thy mortal greatness. Turn thy heart to God, bow the knee, and use the haughty reason to worship him and give him praise.

As one contemplates the scriptures, he thinks of many phrases which describe or characterize God. A few of these are: "Life," "Light," "Truth," "the Way," "Love," "the Creator." All of these terms are dynamic. They are pregnant with meaning. All of them are illustrative of the principle of creativity. That is, regardless of how one thinks of God, in terms of mortal life, resurrection, physical, intellectual, or spiritual illumination, the truth, the means of salvation and exaltation, supreme affection, and so on, the context is always one of potency.

Belonging to the race of God, man is endowed with these same qualities or attributes in some latent or elementary form. God has provided us with the opportunities of mortality that the seeds or rather dormant powers within us may receive stimulation and development and come to full fruition of their possibilities.

In striving to live each day to the fullest and have a full measure of happiness in the process, we must not ever lapse into the notion that life is only a game. For life is serious business, and not only for the here and now but for the anywhere and eternity. If thought of in terms of a game, it must be realized we are playing for keeps and not just for fun.

So, as one strives to apply the revealed word of God to his own life, he should not overlook the multitude of creative dimensions of God and their mortal counterparts in himself, nor should he forget that in all of his efforts to be creative, whatever they are, there is nothing he can do which is greater than strive to help others as well as himself in achieving their and his greatest possibilities which have been made available to him through the endowment from his celestial parentage and the all-important creative act of redemption by the Lord, Jesus Christ.

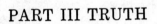

PART III TRUTH

Chapter XIV

TRUTH AND METHOD

The opening sentence of Aristotle's *Metaphysics* is the now famous statement "All men by nature desire to know." The obvious implication is that what man by nature desires to know is the truth. Of all the statements men have recorded about truth it is likely that none is better known than the following one which is attributed to the Lord in the Gospel of John: "And ye shall know the truth, and the truth shall make you free." (John 8:32.) This saying, like many others, is used out of its context perhaps more often than it is used in its context. Knowing the truth is heralded on every hand. Being free is likewise applauded. But the question must be asked, Free from what? I expect most men in our day would rather instantaneously respond by saying free from ignorance. But as Immanuel Kant demonstrated, such a statement is merely an analytical judgment and not a synthetic one for this answer is implicit in the former subject. Knowing the truth implies freedom from ignorance. The Savior's statement means that, but it means much more than that.

When we continue the scripture, to see what it was that the Christ spoke about from which knowledge of the truth would free man, this is what we find, ". . . Verily, verily, I say unto you, Whosoever committeth sin is the servant of sin. . . . If the Son therefore shall make you free, ye shall be free indeed." (John 8:34-36.)

This says very clearly that the freedom Christ had in mind was freedom from sin. Now as we read these verses we find these propositions:

1. Whosoever commits sin is the servant of sin. He is in bondage. (8:34.)

2. If one knows the truth the truth shall make him free. (8:32.)

3. If the Son shall make you free, you shall be free indeed. (8:36.)

Therefore we may conclude that:

The truth is the Son, and,

It is the Son that makes men free.

This conclusion becomes the focal point of the entire gospel. We should note that it is the gospel of Jesus Christ and not the gospel of Elohim, the Father. The gospel and the Church have always borne the name of the Son, and not that of the Father. It was the Son who organized the earth when it was formed. It was the Son who gave commandments to the antediluvian patriarchs. It was the Son who commanded and directed the prophets in ancient Israel. It was the Son who gave vision and revelation to the Prophet Joseph Smith. It is the Son who leads the kingdom today. But, it was the earthly mission of the Son which provided the infinite means of freedom which he offers to all mankind. The two comprehensive freedoms which he offers the family of Adam are freedom from death, and freedom from sin. I called these freedoms comprehensive. Have you ever seriously contemplated the magnitude and meaning of either of them? By revelation we learn that through Jesus' atonement there will be a universal resurrection. No one has to do anything to receive that gift. Resurrection is a free gift.

Even with *this* marvelous gift, however, man might remain in bondage both here and hereafter. But that man might be free from sin, the most heinous of all kinds of bondage, the Christ also provided the means that men might be forgiven of their offenses, through humility and repentance, and therefore liberated from their bondage. Then, we see, he offers us freedom from death and freedom from sin.

Let us recall that the Lord proclaimed himself to be "the way, the truth, and the life." (John 14:6.) No-

tice that here he does not merely say his words are
true, as he does say in some places, but here he declares
I am the truth—I am the truth.

Now as we return to our original verse "Ye shall
know the truth and the truth shall make you free," I believe it will have more meaning. For now we can see
that he who *knows* the Christ is free. Here we must
quote that precious statement from John "And hereby
we do know that we know him, if we keep his commandments." (1 John 2:3.) Keeping his commandments, then, is not only the way to know him, but it is
the way by which we may know that we know him.

The concept of the Christ as the Truth obviously
involves more than temporal implications. With only a
moment's reflection we call to mind that revelation
teaches us that he was a Great Spirit, even a Creator,
before our world was organized. The plan for the redemption of mankind, and for his progression here and
hereafter, was laid in the eternal past, and Jesus the
Son was its Advocate. The plan bore his name. It bears
his name. He is the Redeemer and God of this Earth.
He is the Eternal Truth.

When we think of the Christ as the, or a physical
embodiment, or personification of truth we must remember that there are passages of scripture which refer to his teachings, or the gospel, also as truth.

For example, we have a definition of truth given
by revelation and recorded for us in Section 93 of the
Doctrine and Covenants. It reads: "And truth is knowledge of things as they are, and as they were, and as they
are to come." (Verse 24.) We should notice that according to this definition truth is not an attribute of
things. Ontologically speaking, truth does not belong
to the realm of being. But truth does belong to the realm
of discourse. More simply put things or objects logic-
ally cannot be said to be true or false. Truth and falsity

do not enter until one thing is predicated of another thing. When such a proposition is asserted its congruence with the order of things in the existential world will determine the truth or falsity of the proposition in question.

Notice that in the revelation it does not say truth is things as they are, etc., but it says "truth is the knowledge of things as they are," etc. Here then we see that truth is not the external order of existence. Truth is knowledge. And knowledge is basically organized symbols. Whether the symbols be graphic or phonetic they must be rooted in some kind of concept. And the concept mentioned here is broad in scope. It is not limited to the here and now. Truth is more comprehensive than a mere this and a mere that. It involves an infinite past and an infinite future. Here again we see the plan of God implicit in this revealed definition of truth—his plan of the past, of the present, and for the future. His plan constitutes his truth. When we begin to understand his plan and have some knowledge of things as they are, as they were, and as they are to come, to that extent we have the truth.

When Adam was placed in the garden, he was given the charge to subdue the earth. Since then man has struggled with the elements to sustain himself. From generation to generation what man learned through his experience was passed down to his heirs. The heritage was considerably more than physical goods. The most significant part of it was a body of accumulated experience. This accumulated experience has come to be what we call knowledge. Some have even called it truth. Philosophically, it may have its methodological source in scepticism, authoritarianism, rationalism, empiricism, mysticism, pragmatism, revelation, or in some combination of these. Each of these methods has had its protagonists. Each has been strongly condemned and criticized. Some have believed there are positive characteristics in each of the methods as well as inadequacies or limitation in each of them.

Be that as it may, since the renaissance and the rise of humanism, there has been a predominance of thinkers who have approached the militant in advocating that men study the universe, not only for the joys of understanding and aesthetic appreciation which would come from such study, but that through studying the world she might be known and also exploited.

During recent centuries the method of empiricism seems to have emerged, unquestionably, as a superb means of producing in men new insights into the nature of things. Through the application of its principles men have been able to penetrate many facets of the surface of physical reality.

Perhaps the majority of mankind are little concerned, if at all, with the theoretical aspects of these contributions. The masses of men are more impressed by the physical benefits which come to them personally because of our highly industrialized society with its skilled researchers, designers, engineers, technologists, etc.

Because of the marvelous things which have been revealed, or come to man, through this method, many have enthroned empiricism as the only source of truth and consequently have rejected all other methods. Analogously, one might say, it would be just as reasonable to say, I have eyes and can see, therefore I can abandon my other senses—hearing, smell, taste, and touch. Obviously by such self-imposed limitations one would not be able to grasp the whole of his object. The part that he perceives might be perceived very clearly. But how much more clearly the whole object could be understood had the other available tools been employed rather than condemned and abandoned.

We do not live in a narrow world. We live in a broad and complex world. Its complexity so impressed William James that he called it a multiverse rather than a universe. We need to draw upon all the resources available to us in attempting to understand the order of things.

It is appropriate here to point out with reference to empiricism, that John Dewey, one of its greatest and most influential proponents said, "Science is not constituted by any particular body of subject-matter. It is constituted by a method, a method of changing beliefs by means of tested inquiry as well as of arriving at them. It is its glory, not its condemnation, that its subject-matter develops as the method is improved." (John Dewey, *A Common Faith* [New Haven: Yale University Press, 1947], pp. 38-39.

Science, he says, is a "method of changing beliefs." Furthermore, he says the beliefs are arrived at and changed by tested inquiry. These statements are very important in a consideration of what constitutes truth.

The fact that a belief is arrived at by "tested inquiry" would seem sufficient to label that belief "true." But by the same reasoning if with further "tested inquiry" a new belief is arrived at it too must be designated "true." Consequently, by analysis, and by Dewey's own description, science is a method of changing beliefs. When that is translated into terms of "truth" I believe it would be accurate and consistent to say science is a method of changing truths. Or, as James suggests, it would be better to speak in terms of truer and less true.

My own belief is that we must agree with Dewey when he says of science "It is its glory, not its condemnation, that its subject-matter develops as the method is improved." But the question which naturally presents itself here is, What is the advisability of placing one's total reliance upon a method which admittedly yields beliefs which are impermanent, and changing?

A partial answer to this question may be stated, Reliance upon any method involves a certain amount of confidence or faith in the method itself. In the case of empiricism, if one accepts it for what it is, and for nothing more, all is well. If the empiricist transcends his object and reifies his concepts, he is subject to the antinomies of the rationalist who begins with reason only.

However, just because the empiricist supplants a particular belief with another belief does not necessarily mean that there was no truth value in the first belief. Perhaps the first is subsumed in the second. The subsumption is realized when upon further investigation a more comprehensive view is obtained. Obviously, by means of a theoretical extension of this process it is conceivable that much of the order of existence might be revealed to man. It is appropriate to say here as was said earlier, to the extent that men by this or any other method come to a knowledge of things as they are, as they were, and as they are to come, to that extent will they have arrived at truth.

We recall that Nephi, the son of Lehi, in prophesying said the time would come when some would say ". . . A Bible! A Bible! We have got a Bible, and there cannot be any more Bible. . . . Thou fool, that shall say: A Bible, we have got a Bible, and we need no more Bible." (2 Nephi 29:3, 6.)

I wish to paraphrase these verses as follows: A method! A method! We have got a method, and there cannot be any more method. . . . Thou fool, that shall say: A method, we have got a method, and we need no other method.

Surely John Locke had the right idea when he said ". . . he that takes away reason, to make way for revelation, puts out the light of both, and does much what the

same, as if he would persuade a man to put out his eyes,
the better to receive the remote light of an invisible star
by a telescope." (John Locke, *Essay concerning Human
Understanding*, Book IV, Chapter XIX, paragraph 4.)

All of our faculties are to be used. All of the
methods which man can devise for the obtaining and
promulgation of truth we should employ.

Let us not reject all methods of knowing but one
just because we happen to be familiar with that one.
Let us keep God's commandment to subdue the earth.
And to subdue it we must have knowledge. Let us continue to seek truth and to apply the truth which is already ours.

Here it has been my intent to examine a few of the
many considerations which are involved in Truth. In
summary, this chapter has dealt principally with three
concepts: first, Jesus Christ the Son of God as *the* Truth,
which Truth liberates men from death and sin; and second the definition of truth from The Doctrine and Covenants which indicates that truth as knowledge does not
have the ontological status of the existential world, but
subsists as accurate conceptualizations of the order of
existence. And third, we have briefly discussed empiricism as one of the avenues to truth because of its wide-
spread acceptance today and urged the utilization of all
sources of truth and the recognition of the limitation of
the methods unless they reveal *all* that is, has been, and
will be.

Whether one's life work is academic or non-aca-
demic, he will find the quest discussed here a real one.
It is not a thing for university classes alone. It is a daily
quest in all walks of life. All that one thinks, all that he
says, and all that he does becomes a part of the quest.

One should strive to attend the affairs of his life in
such a way that he will so integrate his intellect, his
passions, and his will, that he will be able to utilize the

potential that is within him and attune himself to the sources of truth which are available to him.

One should never forget this counsel from the Lord:

"And that which doth not edify is not of God, and is darkness. That which is of God is light; and he that receiveth light, and continueth in God, receiveth more light; and that light groweth brighter and brighter until the perfect day." (D&C 50:23-24.)

Chapter XV

EXPERIENCE, REASON AND REVELATION

Experience is a product of intelligence. That is, where there is no intelligence there is no experience. Man's thought and symbol structures reflect intelligence. The simplest word, uttered or written, indicates intelligence. I suppose the essential idea here is found in Descartes' famous "I am" doctrine, "I think, therefore, I am." Experience then requires the existence and presence of an experiencer. We are all experiencers.

Whether or not we as experiencers understand the intricate and delicate inner- and inter-relationships within the functioning processes of our beings, through some of these processes, we all have what can be called an awareness of an external world. That is, outside of the "me" appears to be the "you," and outside of the "you" there appears to be the "me." We, as experiencers, are almost constantly perceiving things external to ourselves. To say that we only experience ideas about things or ideas of the external world, or that all we know, or think we know, is ideas, means very little in a practical way. Surely as we hold an object (say a music box) in our hands and see it with our eyes, and hear it with our ears, we are confident that it is actually in our hands and external to ourselves, although we acknowledge an idea of it within ourselves mediated to us via our sensory apparatus. We have the feeling then, whether one wishes to call it a sensitive or a rational feeling does not matter at the moment, that there is a vast complex of things outside ourselves. As we come into conscious relationships with some of those things, be they experiencer-things or non-experiencer-things, we have what becomes for us an experience. That is, when our sensory apparatus gives us the perception of other persons (experiencers), or material and manufactured things (non-experiencers), and the perception is given conscious attention, then we have an experience. Stimuli from the external world are constantly impinging upon our sensory apparatus but until we give them our attention or they become so strong that they cannot be resisted (as the blast of a horn nearby or the heat from a flame) they are not registered within us, and can hardly be regarded as experiences.

All of the foregoing has dealt with our experience of the external world but we also have experiences which are predominantly reflective.

In fact, it seems to me that all of our experiences may be encompassed or classified within one or more of the following categories: (1) physical, (2) aesthetic, (3) reflective (including intellectual), (4) moral, and (5) religious.

These, then, we may consider the categories of experience. There is probably no experience which belongs exclusively in one category or which in some way does not have elements within it which belong in another category. This means, essentially, that an experience should be classified according to the predominant element within that experience. The predominant element must be determined by the experiencer and therefore involves or reflects in some measure the meaning or interpretation of the experience to the experiencer. It is well to note here that the categories constitute an analytic device only. For, as a matter of fact, the experiences we have are had with a mixture of these elements within them, and our classifying them in one category or another is dependent upon the influence or particular aspect of the experience which impresses us most; for example, when one is particularly entranced by a beautiful sunrise or sunset over the mountains, or across a desert or sea, he has what I would call an aesthetic experience. Upon analysis however, one would have to acknowledge the physical element in the sun, the sky, the mountains, or desert or sea. Hours or days after the experience, as well as at the time of its occurrence, one may enjoy contemplation and then we find the reflective element. For some persons it may provide what they might wish to call a religious experience.

For another example let us consider the appearance of the resurrected Lord to the ten apostles as recorded in the 24th chapter of the Gospel of Luke. The Lord declared that a spirit has not flesh and bones as he had, and invited his disciples to handle him as a witness of his physical being. He likewise asked for food, "And they gave him a piece of a broiled fish, and of an honeycomb. And he took it, and did eat before them." (24:42-43.) Surely this was a physical experience, for to the apostles, the Lord was physically present and gave ample evidence of his identity. But, regardless of the other elements or factors which are to be found in this experience, it seems rather obvious that the best classification, because of the implications, as well as the circumstances per se, is that of religious experience.

We must recognize also that there are some experiences which are predominantly reflective. There are at least three constructive (positive) types within this category. First, there is the enjoyment or satisfaction which comes from recollection or reminiscence. Secondly, there is the intellectual stimulation one may obtain in reading or discussion, etc.; and thirdly, the imagining, or speculating or hypothetical and practical reasoning one may do in an effort to understand better existing or impending circumstances and find means to advance mankind or aid man in achieving noteworthy goals. The range of elements other than the reflective that may be found in what I have suggested, here may extend from the complete unawareness of one's surroundings as he sits comfortably in a lounge chair in deep thought with his eyes closed to one who is in the physical or biological laboratory very much engrossed in apparatus and physical stuff as well as in thought.

Experience includes not only thought and things but also desires, ambitions, sufferings, sorrows, loves, joys, disappointments, and fulfillments. Experience is grounded in life. Rational beings are not only rational, but living, and life involves and requires many things for its fulfillment. Therefore experience is a variegated or complex thing, and we must not let life become subordinate to thought, reason, or intellect, for these must be subordinate to and instruments of the more inclusive category—life. That is, reason does not exhaust life by any means. Thought for the sake of thought may be all right as one proximate end, but thought for the sake of thought can never be the ultimate end.

Now, let us consider reason and its role in experience. Epistemologically speaking, the word "reason" is ordinarily or frequently used as the name of the method which is employed with the source of knowledge termed "rationalism." However, the title "Experience, Reason, and Revelation" is designed to give a broader meaning to the word "reason," as is done not infrequently. In fact, some have used rhetorical and slanted phrases such as "the method of intelligence" to convey their meaning. But there can be little question that throughout the centuries reason has been the citadel of philosophy. Too, it has been the pride of philosophy.

Since the historical beginning of western philosophy reason has been lauded (and sometimes criticized) but particularly from the time of Aristotle's analysis of *anima*, or life or soul, into three levels, the vegetative, sensitive, and the rational, and his definition or description of man as a *rational*, two-footed mammalian, viviparous, animal, living being, this has been the case. As Aristotle found man's rationality to be the characteristic which distinguished him from all other things, he determined that man's virtue or excellence lay in reason. As the saw that cuts well is the good saw and the eye that sees well is the good eye, so the man that reasons well or is truly rational is the good man. We must not overlook the fact that Aristotle taught the now famous golden mean as constituting moral virtue but supreme happiness for him lay not in moral virtue alone but in the higher or intellectual virtue. Be that as it may, reason has continued to be the special claim of all philosophers in the West.

In the sense in which we use the word "reason" here one would probably include rational, empirical, and pragmatic sources of knowledge. That is, sources and methods of knowledge would be included which concern themselves with propositions which are capable of public verification. There can be little equivocation about the potential within these sources of knowlege and methodology (when applied) to increase our awareness of the complexity and intricacies of the world and also our understanding of how to use the stuff of the world. The changes which have been made in the last few centuries, which changes we sometimes call progress, have come about practically by what is called scientific method or, shall we say, reason.

However, as we think of scientific method and/or reason we should be reminded of what Aristotle said about first principles. He observed, and probably indisputably, that basic truths or first principles cannot be demonstrated. For, by definition or description, were they demonstrable they would not be first principles. If they were capable of demonstration the principles used to demonstrate them would be prior to them and more sure than they and would therefore be *more* first, as it were. Obviously, this means that in any field of intellectual endeavor one begins by believing something, or at least acting as though he believes something. Or, to put it differently, one trusts, has confidence in, a faith in, accepts, or believes, certain first principles, or as Aristotle chose to call them, basic truths. This suggests that what we conventionally call knowledge rests upon faith, or belief, or confidence or trust, if some prefer words with fewer religious connotations.

Some persons apparently trust only themselves, their own senses, their own reason, and their own memories. Some philosophers have exalted reason and derogated the senses. Others have rejected (or disparaged) reason and exalted the senses. Still others have found a reputable place for both reason and the senses. Some have embraced reason and mysticism. Some have believed reason to be incompatible with mysticism. But regardless of the source, or combination of sources, of knowledge philosophers have relied upon, each has believed that his own system was reasonable.

And if one thinker charges another with unreasonableness all he really does in essence is say, "What is reasonable to Philosopher X is not consistent with my experience, or my postulates, or there is nothing in my experience to confirm him, therefore, his position is unreasonable to me." The principal criterion of reasonableness then is consistency with experience, or consistency with postulates. Admittedly, there are vast cultural differences in the world and also differences within cultures. Because of these differences, ideas and actions which are accepted as reasonable in some places are regarded as unreasonable in others and vice versa. Who is to say what is true or false, right or wrong, or even better or worse, if reason or reasonableness constitutes the sole criterion?

Certainly this does not mean that we should disregard reason. We must rely upon our reason and experience, but we must make room or some allowance for the experience of others. The further we go in school and the older we get the more dependent we are upon the reliability of others for what we call our knowledge. The student of chemistry or physics does not have time nor does he feel it necessary to perform all of the experiments which have been done by his predecessors. The same is true for the biological student. And the student of history does not have the time nor feel the necessity of searching for all of the historical documents or evidences for the histories he reads. As one reads newspapers, magazines, books, see movies, TV shows, drama, and the events of everyday life, much of what seeps into his mind and gets labeled "knowledge" comes from vicarious experience.

Some of the large libraries of the world have several millions of volumes within them. But if we assume that one began reading a book a week, just one a week, or shall we say fifty books a year, at the age of twenty, and continued that practice until he was eighty, he would have read only three thousand books. And how many persons achieve this? If one should read one book a month during that period he would read only seven hundred and twenty books. How many persons achieve even that? If there were only one million books that could be read, the seven hundred and twenty would be only seven one hundredths of one per cent. Although we only scratch the surface of what men have written, we are still influenced in great measure by what others have done, said, and written. The problem becomes one of choosing what one shall agree with or believe. It is not simply a matter of rejecting all authorities or experts. The authority which is accepted is the one whose ideas or expressions are consistent with the one who chooses. That is, where one who is recognized as an expert or an authority says something which agrees with the experience of a chooser, the latter has no inclination to reject it. The statement is reasonable to him.

But the glory of the method of reason or the method of science, as it is perhaps better known, is testing. Unquestionably, one of the principal differences between ancient and modern science, and one of the reasons for the rapid and almost incredible developments of modern science, is that the ancients were primarily observers of nature, and the moderns are testers or experimenters.

From the time of Aristotle (4 c.B.C.) until that of Galileo (16th and 17th c.A.D.) there was no appreciable progress in the way of scientific knowledge, except in mathematics if one should wish to so classify it, and that was not a western contribution. But Galileo developed an experimental method and used it. Others had written and spoken of experimental science but he *used* experiments and caused a marvelous revolution and from his day until our own there has been one development after another until the acceleration has become so great that the branches of science have become very highly specialized. But with all of the benefits, as we may call them, which have come and, continue to come to us from *these* sources of knowledge, the answers to man's ultimate questions are still wanting. It is true enough that some have reasoned conclusions to those questions, but in this as in other matters reason does not seem to dictate the same answers.

This leads us to a consideration of revelation, the third part of our chapter title. At the outset it must be clearly recognized that belief in revelation requires belief in God. Some people say the believer in God merely assumes there is a God. Can they not in turn be charged with merely assuming there is not God? Furthermore, if they honestly and sincerely want to find out whether there is or is not a God the reasonable thing is to follow the instructions of those who claim to have found him— to have experienced him. The primary ones who have had such experience are the prophets. Many of those who are now dead have left writings. Others are yet among us.

If one believes (or assumes) that God exists, and will follow the counsel of those who have found him, he, too, can find God.

Likewise, if one believes (or assumes) that God does not exist, and does not follow the counsel of those who have found him, he, too, will not find God.

If one is to find God, he must at least want to find him. Some apparently prefer not to find him, feeling that it is easier to assume he does not exist, and they somehow also assume that this relieves them of any allegiance or responsibility to him and will in some way exonerate them if some day in the distant future, even after this life, they find that there really is a post-mortal life and a God after all.

The unbeliever who accuses the believer of assuming the existence of God may be in error because the believer may have found God and experienced him and therefore speak and act from knowledge rather than assumption. And on the contrary, the unbeliever is left only to assume there is no God. So actually, the believer *can* act from knowledge on this matter and the unbeliever from assumption only.

Certainly the prophets are among those who have had experience of, with, or from God. Those experiences are revelations. It is well here to distinguish between revelation and mysticism. Frequently these words are used synonymously, but there seems to be a justifiable and genuine distinction between them. There are two fundamental differences I shall mention. The mystics claim their experiences to be (1) non-sensory and, (2) ineffable. That is, whatever their experiences are they are immediate; they are not mediated via the senses. And also their experiences are ineffable, or indescribable. There is no specific communication that is received beyond the feeling produced within the mystic that all is eternal. But in the cases of the prophets their experiences have been sensory and communicable. The senses of sight, hearing, and touch have all been employed and sometimes two or three simultaneously. Furthermore, the prophets have stated what they have experienced and sometimes in great simplicity.

To some, then, revelation has been and is a source of knowledge. It has been and is more than reading a book written by predecessors or contemporaries. And thus to those who experience it, it is something dynamic and real and reliable.

Some have chosen to deny revelation because they have never recognized any in their own lives. But just because one person does not receive revelation is certainly no reason to deny that others have it.

Too, although revelation is generally private experience, that makes it no less real. Or to say that revelation is subjective does not condemn it, for what experience is not subjective? By the very nature of experience, if it is not personal or subjective, it is not experience. Surely it is recognized that revelation is not the kind of experience that can be reproduced at will as a demonstration for the unbeliever. But we should remember that even in the case of the physically demonstrable one must at least be willing to test a proposition. So in the realm of that which is not publicly verifiable or demonstrable one must at least be willing to test a proposition. For testing produces testimony.

In conclusion let me say, rationalism, empiricism, pragmatism, authoritarianism (the opinions of the experts), all have their place and perform useful and necessary functions within the lives of men. These sources and methods supplement and complement one another in giving men knowledge, just as the various crafts supplement and complement one another in giving men dwellings. But no one of these human sources of knowledge, or any combination of them, has been able to give man knowledge of ultimate things. For that knowledge we are dependent upon revelation. And there are those who have had revelation in the past, and there are those who do have revelation at the present—men who are sound in body and in mind. Certainly they are men who are as reliable as those who would deny and even ridicule such claims. And surely denial and ridicule in no way change the fact of communication from man to God and from God to man.

And where there are those who in the pride of their own intellects or reason, will not humble themselves sufficiently to recognize their own finitude, and honestly and perseveringly strive to find God by heeding the counsel of the prophets, they apparently find themselves estranged from the spirit of revelation and are left to satisfy what yearnings they may have by the exercise of their own feeble reason. For as strong and capable as men's minds appear to be in some things, when it comes to the ultimate things no one mortal mind, nor any group of them, has been able to learn and know those things which God has chosen to reserve to be revealed according to his will. So, if one, anyone, wishes that knowledge, the way is available for him to obtain it, and that way he must learn from the prophets, those who have found it. For as Paul wrote to the Corinthians, we know the things of man by the spirit of man and the things of God by the Spirit of God.

Chapter XVI

SOME METAPHYSICAL REFLECTIONS ON THE GOSPEL OF JOHN

Introduction

Those persons with even the barest acquaintance with the Gospels know that each is an account of the earthly life and ministry of Jesus Christ. This fact being true, it is natural to expect that Jesus would be the central subject of the Gospels. The preface to the Gospel of John is a superb example of the centrality of Jesus in those books.

Through the years I have been aware of these facts, but upon my most recent reading and studying the Gospel of John the extent of Jesus' centrality in that book was impressed upon me with far greater rational force than ever before. I am not speaking here of a testimony of Jesus as the Christ—that is another matter. I am speaking of the Gospel of John as a book and the place of Jesus in that book.

It is interesting that the force of my realization came during the process of a metaphysical inquiry rather than during what might be distinguished as theological or doctrinal study. Of course, I have devoted considerable time to the study of doctrine, and I acknowledge my indebtedness to God for the witness of the Spirit that Jesus is the Christ. However, the point that I want to make is that as one reads John's Gospel with metaphysical concepts in mind it is most revealing to see how completely everything is oriented in the Lord; for example, some of the categories one might consider are being, becoming, relation, potency, unity, duality, teleology, change, process, and causation. Let me offer three brief illustrations and some general observations.

Being

First, let us consider perhaps the most basic of all philosophic concepts, being. This word is the noun form of the verb "to be." "To be" ordinarily means "to exist." For something to exist or to be means that it is. In case the "it" happens to refer to a person one would more properly say he is. The comparable form in the first person singular is I am. This is the name Jesus used in an encounter with the Jews who claimed to identify themselves with Abraham. In maintaining his priority to Abraham, Jesus said, "Before Abraham was, I am." (John 8:58.) Here Jesus referred to himself in the same language used in the revelation to Moses at the burning bush: "I AM THAT I AM. . . . Thus shalt thou say to the children of Israel, I AM hath sent me unto you." (Exodus 3:14.) Of course, this statement has the force of saying, I am he who is.

Jesus used the phrase "I am" in many statements to his disciples, in John's book. We all use the phrase "I am" extensively; however, the "I am" statements of Jesus are of great ontological significance; for example, he says to the Samaritan woman regarding the Messiah, "I that speak unto thee am he." (John 4:26.) To others he said, "I am the bread of life" (*Ibid.*, 6:35), "I am the living bread" (*Ibid.*, 6:51), "I am the light of the world" (*Ibid.*, 8:12), "I am the door of the sheep" (*Ibid.*, 10:7), "I am the resurrection, and the life" (*Ibid.*, 11:25), "Ye call me Master and Lord: and ye say well; for so I am" (*Ibid.*, 13:13), "I am the way, the truth, and the life" (*Ibid.*, 14:6), and "I am the vine, ye are the branches." (*Ibid.*, 15:5.)

Implicit in all of these statements is the idea that Jesus has a secure ontological status. He, in his own being, is living bread, light, the door, the resurrection, the life, the way, the truth, the vine, the Lord, the Master, the Messiah.

Of course, the preface to John's Gospel, already alluded to, relates importantly to what I am saying. It identifies Jesus as the Word, who was made flesh, and dwelled among men (*Ibid.*, 1:14), and as he who made all things. (*Ibid.*, 1:3.) Also the preface says, "In him was life; and the life was the light of men." (*Ibid.*, 1:4.)

These statements are consistent with the others just cited which come from various parts of John's Gospel on the point that being is in some way inherent in Jesus. Of Jesus, to say he is, is not enough, for "isness" in Jesus implies so many things beyond mere existence. Jesus not merely is, he is God. To be is one thing, to be God is quite another. As stated earlier, we all say, "I am;" Jesus said, "I am he."

The priority of Jesus is asserted by John in the opening sentences of his book. He said: "In the beginning was the Word, and the Word was with God, and the Word was God. The same was in the beginning with God." (*Ibid.*, 1:1-2.) Therefore, from the outset John identifies Jesus as the Word, says that he was with God in the beginning, and that he was God. And then, as it were, to be sure that although Jesus is God, he would not be confused with the Father, he repeated, "The same was in the beginning with God." (*Ibid.*, 1:2.)

Obviously, there are many implications regarding God, the universe, and man in the foregoing, but my concern here has been to explore very briefly being as it relates to Jesus. One of the very fascinating dimensions of the foregoing, being and Jesus, introduces another metaphysical category, that of relation. One of the most interesting aspects of this category is the relation of Jesus to the Father.

Relation

As is well-known, the substantial relation of Jesus and the Father was a matter of philosophical and theological controversy for centuries. I have no intention

of entering that controversy here. However, there are
a few matters having to do with the functional relation
between the Father and Son, which are also of an ontological character, I wish to mention.

In what I have already said I have indicated that
in John's Gospel Jesus is the central subject, he is I
am, *being* as it were; and yet, in addition to all of the
"I am" statements of Jesus, he is represented as continuously paying filial homage to the one who sent him
—the Father; for example, he said: "For I came down
from heaven, not to do mine own will, but the will of him
that sent me." (*Ibid.*, 6:38.) Also, "My doctrine is not
mine, but his that sent me." (*Ibid.*, 7:16.) Finally, "My
meat is to do the will of him that sent me, and to finish
his work." (*Ibid.*, 4:34; see also *ibid.*, 6:29; 6:44-45; 7:
28-29; 10:36; 12:44; 13:20; 17:3.)

Other passages illustrate dimensions of the filial
homage in Jesus. He declared ". . . for my Father
is greater than I." (*Ibid.*, 14:28.) In another place he had
said, "My Father . . . is greater than all." (*Ibid.*, 10:29.)
". . . As my Father hath taught me, I speak these things."
(*Ibid.*, 8:28.) "I speak that which I have seen with my
Father: and ye do that which ye have seen with your
father." (*Ibid.*, 8:38.) But Jesus is not only represented
as acknowledging his Father as Father, but also he acknowledges him as his God. In giving instructions to
Mary Magdalene, he said, ". . . go to my brethren, and
say unto them, I ascend unto my Father, and your
Father; and to my God, and your God." (*Ibid.*, 20:17.)

These passages regarding the functional relation
between the Father and the Son perhaps illumine what
was said earlier about the I am statements. The essence
of all those statements seems to be best expressed in the
phrase, "I am the way, the truth, and the life" (*Ibid.*,
14:6), and in the words, "I am the door of the sheep."
(*Ibid.*, 10:7.) That is, as I am, Jesus is not only *being*

as such, but he is the "door," the "way," etc., to God, his Father. He pays homage to God as his Father and as his God, yet at the same time he, Jesus, is I am, and central to John's Gospel as the sole means of man's ever returning to God. At this point obviously, the question of the relation of the Father and the Son to man arises, but this question will necessarily have to be ignored here as much as possible in the interest of space.

The I am statements are a few of the many assertions that Jesus is the only way to the Father. Illustrating both this point and that about filial homage is this widely quoted verse: "For God so loved the world, that he gave his only begotten Son, that whosoever believeth in him should not perish, but have everlasting life." (*Ibid.*, 3:16.) John quotes Jesus often regarding this matter. Jesus said: "This is the work of God, that ye believe on him whom he hath sent." (*Ibid.*, 6:29.) This clearly identifies the work of God as belief in Jesus. But Jesus being the "way" or "door" to God he said: "He that believeth on me, believeth not on me, but on him that sent me." (*Ibid.*, 12:44.) Similarly, ". . . he that receiveth me receiveth him that sent me." (*Ibid.*, 13:20.) These statements seem to be sufficiently lucid that anyone should be able to grasp the point that one functional relation of Jesus to the Father is that he is the only means by which men can return to the Father. The statements or verses quoted are formulated positively. There is another statement formulated negatively which John attributes to Jesus which is probably far more emphatic regarding the relation under discussion than any other. Jesus said: "He that hateth me hateth my Father also." (*Ibid.*, 15:23.) This strikes sharply at those persons who would profess belief in God and reject Jesus. Simply put, those who hate Jesus hate God also. Here is a rather summary verse on this relation of Jesus and the Father: "And this is life eternal, that they might know thee the only true God, and Jesus Christ, whom thou hast sent." (*Ibid.*, 17:3.) In summary, it appears Jesus was God who was with God from the beginning. He was the Creator who saw what his Father did, was taught by him, became his only begotten Son, obeyed his commandments (*Ibid.*, 14:31; 15:10), identified himself as the only way men could return to God, and declared that eternal life involved knowing both God the Father and himself. The metaphysical question of relation in the Godhead involves a number of other questions, the most obvious of which, perhaps, being those of unity, duality, and trinity. These are rooted in such familiar verses as, "I and my Father are one" (*Ibid.*, 10:30), "Believe me that I am in the Father, and the Father in me" (*Ibid.*, 14:11), ". . . when the Comforter is come, whom I will send unto you from the Father . . . he shall testify of me" (*Ibid.*, 15:26), etc. (See also, *ibid.*, 10:38; 14:11; 14:20; and 17:21.) Up to this point we have attempted to examine briefly certain aspects of two metaphysical issues; Jesus and being, and the functional relation between Jesus and the Father.

Duality

Now let us look even more briefly at another metaphysical category manifested in several aspects of John's Gospel. That is duality. There are three basic dualisms in what might be called the metaphysics of John's Gospel. These dualisms may be designated appropriately, condition or state, process, and end. These three categories are interrelated, for the first, condition or state, has to do with things as they are; the second, process, has to do with the becoming of things in one of the two conditions or states; and the third, ends, concerns the consequences of the processes which are operative on things in one of the two conditions or states.

As regards the first category, condition or state, we observe John representing Jesus as contrasting his mortal environment with his pre-mortal environment. He speaks of earthly things and heavenly things. (*Ibid.*, 3: 12.) Jesus said: ". . . he that is of the earth is earthly, and speaketh of the earth: he that cometh from heaven is above all." (*Ibid.*, 3:31.) Speaking to the Pharisees, he charged: "Ye are from beneath; I am from above: ye are of this world; I am not of this world." (*Ibid.*, 8: 23.) The entire context of this passage is an illustration of this dualism. One aspect of it may be an extension of the earthly contrasted with the heavenly, or only a more vigorous and graphic formulation of the same dualism. I am inclined toward the latter interpretation. In Jesus' verbal exchange with the Pharisees they claimed Abraham as their father. Jesus said: "Ye are of your father the devil, and the lusts of your father ye will do," etc. (*Ibid.*, 8:44.) Then he said, "He that is of God heareth God's words: ye therefore hear them not, because ye are not of God." (*Ibid.*, 8:47.) Here Jesus' expression "earthly things" becomes sufficiently inclusive to include men. The earthly things and heavenly things dualism becomes a "Ye are of your father the devil" and "I am of my Father, God" dualism. (See *Ibid.*, 8:38-47.) In this dualism, however, all men were not considered earthly, as were the Pharisees alluded to here. Of Jesus' disciples, in a prayer to his Father and God, he said: ". . . and the world hath hated them, because they are not of the world, even as I am not of the world." (*Ibid.*, 17:14.) What we see then, fundamentally, is that, according to John's Gospel, of the things that are (speaking with a grammatical interest), or (speaking with a metaphysical interest) of the things that be, some are in a condition or state called earthly and others are in the condition or state called heavenly. As regards being *per se*, ontologically this is a dualism.

Process in John's Gospel is the second example of dualism. Process has to do with the becoming of those who are mortal. Jesus speaks of two potencies in process and these constitute the processive bifurcation. He said: "It is the spirit that quickeneth; the flesh profiteth nothing." (*Ibid.*, 6:63.) Also he said, "Labour not for the meat which perisheth, but for that meat which endureth unto everlasting life, which the Son of man shall give unto you." (*Ibid.*, 6:27.) Therefore, as there is a fundamental dualism of conditions or states, earthly and heavenly, there is a fundamental dualism of process, spirit and flesh. But man does not remain mortal man. Process, whichever one is operative in the case of a given individual, gives rise to consequences. This statement brings us to the third dualism in the metaphysics of John's Gospel, ends.

Simply put, what we have here is this. First there is being; something exists; more specifically, man is. Second, not only is man; he is in a process—that is, he is active and being acted upon; or, putting it otherwise, not only is man, but he is going, or more technically, becoming. Third, not only is man, and is he going, or becoming, but he is going somewhere or becoming something. The point is, the processes result in ends. Jesus speaks of two ends, a dualism of ends; for example, he said, "He that believeth on the Son hath everlasting life: and he that believeth not the Son shall not see life; but the wrath of God abideth on him." (*Ibid.*, 3: 36.) Perhaps the statement which is as clear as any in John on this point is where Jesus was reported speaking on the eventual judgment of all mankind by himself, the Son, and he said: ". . . for the hour is coming, in the which all that are in the graves shall hear his voice, And shall come forth; they that have done good, unto the resurrection of life; and they that have done evil, unto the resurrection of damnation." (*Ibid.*, 5:28-29.) The dualism of ends is clearly distinguished as everlasting life and the wrath of God, or even more clearly, as the resurrection of life and the resurrection of damnation. So, in the condition or state of being, in process, and also in ends, in John's Gospel, we find dualisms.

In this brief chapter I have attempted to point out some of the metaphysical aspects of the fourth Gospel. Summarily, we have examined three basic concepts, being, relation, and duality. We considered being as it applies to Jesus, relation as it applies functionally between the Father and the Son, and duality as it is found in terms of condition or state of being, process, and ends.

There are other fascinating metaphysical concepts in the light or perspective of which the Johannine Gospel might be examined, such as unity, teleology, causation, change, and especially potency, but my study of that book in those terms, as well as those discussed in this chapter, sustains the basic thesis of the entire Christian enterprise, that as far as man is concerned all things are oriented in Jesus the Christ.

Chapter XVII

"YE SHALL KNOW THE TRUTH . . ."

The Lord said, ". . . ye shall know the truth, and the truth shall make you free." (John 8:32.) Probably there is no verse of scripture which has been taken out of context and been given private interpretation more frequently than this verse. It is granted that when this verse has no context but is isolated the apparent meaning is an appealing one. I suppose it is accurate to say that this is particularly true for the academician—the scholar and the scientist. I likewise suppose there is a sense of mission and a special kind of satisfaction which comes to one who feels he is engaged in an enterprise which makes men free. Furthermore, I believe there is a general sense in which knowing the truth does make one free. This has been one of the fundamental assumptions of the advocates of liberal education. But after one has said this, and a host of other things which might be said in defense of the isolated statement "Ye shall know the truth, and the truth shall make you free," what can be said for the nature of the freedom which is envisioned here? Regardless of how else this freedom might be described, I think it can be asserted with considerable confidence that its primary benefits are temporal, that is, they belong to this world. Or, putting it another way, there are many who think of man's existence as being limited to mortality and therefore their aspirations are to make man free during the only existence they think he has. There are others who do not conceive of man's life as being limited to mortality but who apparently obtain a special kind of solace in the hope that their academic knowledge, or knowledge of the world, may be the means of their obtaining freedom in their post-mortal existence. We are not altogether free of those who hold this view. I shall return to this point later.

Now, if this common interpretation of this passage, stripped of its context, is not what the Lord meant by the quoted words, just what did he mean?

When one reads the Lord's words in their context it becomes clear that he was not speaking of truth in the abstract general sense which I have just described. On the contrary, he was speaking specifically. In the first place he was speaking "to those Jews which believed on him." In the second place he said, "If ye continue in my word, then are ye my disciples indeed," and then thirdly he promised "And ye shall know the truth and the truth shall make you free." (See *ibid.*, 8:31-32.) So the truth to make men free was promised to those who believed on him, but further, only to those who believed on him who continued in his word.

But, what did the Lord mean by the word "truth"? As he continued his explanation he said, "If the Son therefore shall make you free, ye shall be free indeed." (*Ibid.*, 8:36.) It is obvious that he was equating himself with the truth, as he did at least on one other occasion when he said, "I am the way, the truth, and the life." (*Ibid.*, 14:6.)

Further examination of the context under discussion, as well as many others, makes it evident that the freedom man was assured through the truth, namely Jesus Christ the Lord, was freedom from sin and freedom from death. These constitute freedoms of incomparable magnitude, freedoms which knowledge, in and of itself, is utterly helpless to yield.

Jesus, in his classic misused statement, has a concept of truth and freedom that is ultimate in its meaning and significance, and infinitely beyond the proximate, but sometimes hopeful, meaning and significance, given it by perhaps well-meaning but misinformed or uninspired men.

There is a marked tendency among men to dissociate truth and Jesus. Sometimes even among the Latter-day Saints there are those who in emphasizing the breadth of the gospel somehow seem to forget that it is the gospel of Jesus Christ. The Lord has been sufficiently emphatic regarding his identification with the gospel. The gospel bears his name; the Church bears his name; he was the Creator of this earth; he is Jehovah, the God of the Old Testament; he is the Redeemer, and also the great Judge. We have been told to do all that we do in his name. We must not forget that when we speak of truth in any ultimate sense it cannot be dissociated from Jesus Christ.

One may speak of truth in some abstract absolute philosophic sense and revel in his discoveries which may approximate that truth, but then what? As I said above, there may be and are distinct temporal advantages which accrue to man in the pursuit and acquisition of truth in this general abstract sense, but in order for one to be free, in any ultimate sense, he must come to know the truth, that is, Jesus Christ the Lord.

In addition to speaking of himself as truth the Lord also refers to his word, or his gospel, as truth. That is, in addition to his power as the Redeemer over sin and death and therefore the truth or power which frees man, the everlasting principles which are for man's benefit in his striving to become like the Lord, and his and our Father, come from him who is truth and therefore they are denominated truth. More simply put, the word "truth" is applied by the Lord both to himself and to principles.

Mankind ordinarily uses the word in a way somewhat related to the second usage of the Lord. Technically, truth is regarded as a characteristic of propositions. That is to say, truth does not belong to things but to statements or propositions. Things simply are; they are not true or false. This point is made rather clearly in a revelation to the Prophet Joseph Smith in which we find, "And truth is knowledge of things as they are, and as they were, and as they are to come." (D&C 93:24.) So truth is not things as they are, were, and will be, but truth is knowledge of things as they are, were, and will be. Things are what they are, were, and will be, regardless of what men believe or say about them.

If we consider truth in this propositional sense it is well for us to make a distinction. It is an assumption, but one with which I believe most, if not all, men will agree, that all true propositions are not of equal value. That is to say, all truths are not of equal value. They range in worth from the trivial to the sublime. They may be classified in various ways. However, perhaps the most important classification is to recognize that some truths are secular and others are redemptive.

To call some truths secular does not mean they are valueless. It means they have a different value from those called redemptive. We know secular truths do have value for mortals. They may have value for post-mortals, and probably do, but to what extent they are needed we do not know. Redemptive truths have value not only for mortals but are essential for post-mortals if they are to fulfill the true purpose of their being.

From near the beginning of man's sojourn on earth he has sought secular and redemptive knowledge. Adam was told that the earth was cursed for the man's sake or benefit, and he was commanded to subdue it. From that time man has struggled in his so-called pursuit of truth in trying not merely to understand but to overcome nature to make his lot easier. Also Adam, after manifest faithfulness, was given knowledge of redemptive truth. Since that time man has had his ups and downs in pursuit of redemptive truth.

We declare in all soberness that the gospel of Jesus Christ has been restored to the earth through personal manifestations of the Father and the Son, and a host of other beings, and yet there are those among us who are so enraptured with the so-called pursuit of knowledge that they exult in the choice revelations of the Lord regarding knowledge, and at the same time minimize the very existence of the Father and the Son to the point not only of neglect in acknowledging them, but to the point of seeming embarrassment if not disgust if others mention them.

In the Doctrine and Covenants there are some glorious passages which admonish man to seek knowledge; for example:

Teach ye diligently and my grace shall attend you, that you may be instructed more perfectly in theory, in principle, in doctrine, in the law of the gospel, in all things that pertain unto the kingdom of God, that are expedient for you to understand;

Of things both in heaven and in the earth, and under the earth; things which have been, things which are, things which must shortly come to pass; things which are at home, things which are abroad; the wars and the perplexities of the nations, and the judgments which are on the land; and a knowledge also of countries and of kingdoms— (D&C 88:78-79.)

As one reads these two verses experience suggests that it is natural for him to begin immediately to identify certain recognized academic disciplines. The next step is for him to assume that the knowledge in these disciplines is saving knowledge, that is, either assures him of, or strongly contributes to his chance of being saved in God's kingdom.

However, if such an one should read the next verse he would discover he had erred in his interpretation of the previous verses. The passage continues:

That ye may be prepared in all things when I shall send you again to magnify the calling whereunto I have called you, and the mission with which I have commissioned you. (*Ibid.*, 88:80.)

The Lord makes it quite clear that the purpose for one's learning the things suggested in the other verses is that he might be better prepared to accomplish the purposes of the Lord.

Here is another frequently quoted verse:

And set in order the churches, and study and learn, and become acquainted with all good books, and with languages, tongues, and people. (*Ibid.*, 90:15.)

Here again is a passage which is often used to suggest that, after all, becoming acquainted with all good books, with languages, tongues, and people are in and of themselves means of salvation. Once more, the advocate of such a view should read on, for he would find the Lord saying to the Prophet Joseph Smith and his counselors:

And this shall be your business and mission in all your lives, to preside in council, and set in order all the affairs of this church and kingdom. (*Ibid.*, 90:16.)

The purpose of their studying good books, languages, etc. was that the Prophet Joseph Smith and his Counselors might be prepared to more efficiently and effectively build the kingdom of God for the salvation of God's children.

Examples of this kind could be multiplied, for throughout the scriptures as God counsels his children to seek knowledge it is always for the express purpose of being better prepared to do his will.

A corollary of this misuse of the scriptures concerning knowledge is the deceiver I call the gospel of success. Deep in our national culture as well as deep in our religious culture is the concept of industry. Nurtured on the concept that this was a country of free men with all of the natural resources a beneficent God could bestow upon a people it was only natural that men should give rise to the concept which in turn would become equally prevalent that any man who was industrious could become a success. From childhood we are taught in this American culture that if we work hard, apply ourselves with mind and might, we can really become somebody; we can become wealthy, or famous, or even the President of our country. There are hosts of wonderful success stories which stir young and old alike.

Certainly it is not my intent to discourage anybody from working, or being industrious. However, when one's work, his vocation or profession, and all of his industrious effort is expended in the acquisition of temporal goods, possessions, and positions, there is cause for alarm.

During the last fifty years the worldly fortune of the Latter-day Saints has changed. Already there is a list of names of considerable size of Latter-day Saints who have been successful in the world. I am sure we are grateful and happy for their achievement and recognition. More and more the young people of the Church, and particularly of the university, are becoming acquainted with the names of these successful persons and in some cases have the good fortune to see and hear these persons themselves. Inasmuch as most of the "successful" Latter-day Saints about whom we hear are active members of the Church, and inasmuch as they frequently attribute their success in the world to being a member of the Church, there is the implication that if one is a good member of the Church he will be a success in the world. And, irrespective of the reasoning, whether valid or invalid, the reverse of the conclusion is assumed to follow, namely, if a member of the Church is a success in the world he is a good Latter-day Saint. Both of these conclusions are false. Being a good member of the Church is no guarantee of worldly success. There are many wonderful folk worthy of the name Latter-day Saint who have achieved little by the standards of the world. Likewise, worldly success is not certain evidence of one's worthiness before the Lord.

We cannot afford to be seduced by the glamorous appeal of worldly success to become so enthralled with her charms that we permit ourselves to be lulled into the belief that worldly success is synonymous with the gospel. Everyone should work, and work hard, but in all of his striving he should never cease to be actively conscious that God is very probably not nearly so aware of and pleased with his worldly accomplishments as are he and his mother.

It seems to me that there are three kinds of success. I have been speaking of worldly success, but I believe this can be divided into two kinds. The first I call success of the body. Much of man's endeavor as a mortal is devoted to acquiring those things which satisfy the needs and desires of the body. To the extent that one is able to obtain the means to satisfy those needs and desires, to that extent he achieves success of the body. This kind of success is primarily proportional to one's economic success.

The second kind, which I consider a division of worldly success, I call success of the spirit. By the word "spirit" I do not refer to the spirit being which is tabernacled in mortal bodies, nor do I mean those things which Latter-day Saints generally consider enduring or eternal. On the contrary, inasmuch as I am describing a kind of worldly success, I use the word "spirit" here to conform more closely to the kinds of things which seem more and more extensively meant by or associated with this word, that is, I am giving it temporal limitations. It is maintained that not only does man, as man, have basic physical needs but he has some basic psychic needs

also, for example, the need to belong, the need for love
and affection, the need for acceptance and recognition,
and others, including what Aristotle and other philosophers have called a natural desire to know. To the extent that one is able to satisfy these and similar needs,
to that extent he achieves success of spirit.

Fundamentally what I have included here in success of the body and success of the spirit are those things
which belong to this world, even the most positive things
which men cultivate without God. For the Lord himself
has said in our day:

And everything that is in the world, whether it be ordained of men, by thrones, or principalities, or powers, or
things of name, whatsoever they may be, that are not by me or
by my word, saith the Lord, shall be thrown down, and shall not
remain after men are dead, neither in nor after the resurrection, saith the Lord your God. (*Ibid.*, 132:13.)

Or, as the Lord warned his disciples against the
false teachings of the Pharisees,

Every plant, which my heavenly Father hath not planted,
shall be rooted up. (Matthew 15:13.)

It is granted that many things have value for man
and give him satisfaction in this life. As a matter of
fact, many of the things involved in success of the body
and success of the spirit are essential to mortal existence, and must therefore be had in some degree by all
men. However, there are increasing numbers of men
and women who at least in act have denied anything else
and have completely given themselves to mortality. But
the important thing each person should ask himself, in
the words of the Lord, is, what kinds of plants am
I planting, cultivating, and nurturing? Will my harvest, if I have one, be mortal? Will all of the plants I
cultivate eventually be rooted up? Will all of my efforts, and I, come to naught? Or, am I planting those

plants which will bear eternal fruit and find a glorious fulfillment in my soul? Everyone makes the choice.

In one of the revelations of the Lord he declared, "And the spirit and the body are the soul of man." (D&C 88:15.) This statement from the Lord gives rise to my third kind of success, success of the soul. All of God's children stand in need of understanding certain principles which God has revealed expressly for their welfare. Not only must the principles be understood but they must be applied to produce the effects which are needed in the lives of men.

Consistent with what was said above regarding truth, secular and redemptive, or temporal and eternal, one may achieve remarkable success of the body and success of the spirit in this life without achieving success of the soul, but their having been won, then what? Certainly we would wish for every man, success of the body, success of the spirit, and success of the soul. We are concerned with man's temporal and eternal well-being. When we declare we are working for the salvation of the souls of men, it means we are striving to save the bodies of men as well as their spirits. Success of the soul in the lives of mortals manifests itelf in living in the world without being of the world. We must overcome the world, as the Savior said. But we must not mistake "overcome" to mean triumph over the world in terms of worldly success.

The following verses from the revelation of the Lord in Section 50 of the Doctrine and Covenants bear on this point.

. . . why is it that ye cannot understand and know, that he that receiveth the word by the Spirit of truth receiveth it as it is preached by the Spirit of truth?

Wherefore, he that preacheth and he that receiveth, understand one another, and both are edified and rejoice together.

And that which doth not edify is not of God, and is darkness.

That which is of God is light; and he that receiveth light, and continueth in God, receiveth more light; and that light groweth brighter and brighter until the perfect day. (*Ibid.*, 50:21-24.)

There are many things worthy of comment in these precious lines, however, I shall only emphasize a point from the last verse. "That which is of God is light; and he that receiveth light and continueth in God, receiveth more light." Remember, the Lord has told us that he is the light, and his principles are also called the light. (*Ibid.*, 6:21, John 1.) In this verse he declares "he that receiveth light," etc. He says "receiveth," not ignoreth, not amendeth, not quibbleth about, not is embarrassed about, not rejecteth, but receiveth, and "receiveth" means to take into one's possession, to make one's own. "Receiveth" here implies much more than intellectual assent. The structure of the passage suggests emotional and volitional assent as well. Thus, he that receiveth the light, and continueth in God, receiveth more light, and reciprocally as the light grows brighter and brighter the individual more and more overcomes the world and achieves success of the soul.

There seems to be an additional meaning, or, should I say, application of the word "light." In an oft-quoted verse of scripture the Lord says, "The glory of God is intelligence." (D&C 93:36.) This is certainly a beautiful statement, one which immediately finds lodgment in the mind of one who loves the things of the mind. Aristotle's conception of philosophic wisdom and Spinoza's intellectual love of God cannot compare with it. But that is not the complete passage. It reads:

The glory of God is intelligence, or, in other words, light and truth.
Light and truth forsake that evil one. (*Ibid.*, 93:36-37.)

In view of what the scriptures say regarding light and truth it is evident that by "intelligence" the Lord does not mean knowledge of encyclopedic proportions. Here in using the word "intelligence" it appears that again the Lord is not speaking merely of what men call the processes of thinking, but also includes the processes of feeling and doing. Or, to put it differently, it appears to me the Lord is saying the glory of God is celestial character, for celestial character forsakes that evil one. Yes, man needs knowledge, here and hereafter, but regardless of how much knowledge he has he needs intelligence—character.

For example, the Lord has said:

Whatever principle of intelligence we attain unto in this life, it will rise with us in the resurrection.

And if a person gains more knowledge and intelligence in this life through his diligence and obedience than another, he will have so much the advantage in the world to come. (*Ibid.*, 130:18-19.)

Consistent with the foregoing, and for the purpose of trying to understand this passage more clearly, let us use the word "character" for "intelligence."

Here it may be helpful to recall that in a glorious revelation to Abraham God referred to man's basic and original being as an intelligence—an intelligence. (Abraham 3:18-23.) What I am proposing here is that regardless of man's state, as an intelligence, a premortal spirit, a mortal, a post-mortal spirit, or a resurrected being, that which he *is* at any given time may be called his character. Therefore, I am not using the word "intelligence" to mean learning, nor even wisdom, as usually conceived, for these are particular characteristics, whereas character means that which one really is.

With this concept in mind the passage reads: "Whatever principle of *character* we attain unto in this life, it will rise with us in the resurrection." Or, putting it in other words, whatever we become in soul, that is precisely what we will be in the resurrection. And continuing, "And if a person gains more knowledge and character in this life through his diligence and obedience than another, he will have so much the advantage in the world to come."

It is obvious in this verse that the Lord is talking about something more than knowledge, for he speaks of knowledge *and* intelligence (or character), and it is clearly evident throughout the revelations that God's primary concern with man is not with what he knows but what he is.

On one occasion the Prophet Joseph Smith declared "A man is saved no faster than he gets knowledge, . . ." (*DHC* 4:588.) This statement, too, has been taken out of its context often and used to support a "knowledge for the sake of knowledge" concept, or a "knowledge is salvation" doctrine. No one should permit himself to fall into such an error. Knowledge for the sake of knowledge is a phrase which may have meaning in some formal empty sense. Perhaps the closest thing to knowledge for the sake of knowledge which is significant is what is called pure research, an endeavor in which one is not concerned about uses or application of the principles discovered or formulated, but solely with finding out that which was formerly unknown. But even here the phrase is not accurately applicable, for the searcher is not in pursuit of knowledge for the sake of knowledge, he is in pursuit of knowledge for the sake of satisfying some hunger or thirst he has for knowledge. The same principle obtains in the case of so-called art for the sake of art, and even virtue for the sake of virtue.

Fundamentally, all three of these for the sake of's have the same form and have real meaning only when it is realized that their basic structure is knowledge, or art, or virtue, for the sake of value. That is, they are not knowledge for the sake of knowledge, nor art for the

sake of art, nor virtue for the sake of virtue, but each
for the sake of value. For value, that is, values, are for
persons, and must not be abstractly conceived as independent of or divorced from persons, but acknowledged
by and grounded in persons. (Values have a logical being all their own, but that is another matter.) Here
value is not conceived in any economic or instrumental
sense, but in the sense that persons are motivated to
pursue them, in knowledge, art, or virtue, on the assumption that there is intrinsic value in the pursuit and
in its consequences. But even though we speak of intrinsic value it is always value for persons.

We must not be deceived and believe that when the
Prophet Joseph Smith said, "A man is saved no faster
than he gets knowledge," he meant knowledge per se.
The context from which this statement comes makes this
plain. But as we are tempted to equate knowledge with
salvation let us remember the mighty Lucifer, one who
had and has great knowledge, probably knowledge beyond our present capacity to imagine. Yet that great
knowledge is not going to save him, but on the contrary
it has been already the means of persuading one-third
of God's children to forsake their Father, and is still being use to dissuade God's mortal children to forsake
him. Knowledge is necessary, but knowledge is not
enough! Knowledge and intelligence (character) will
rise with us in the resurrection.

The Prophet Joseph Smith also received a revelation which included the words "It is impossible for a
man to be saved in ignorance." (DHC 5:392. D&C 131:
6.) These words, as others previously discussed, have
been used extensively to encourage people to seek excellence in the traditional academic disciplines with the
express intent that these were the things of which man
could not be ignorant and be saved. And yet the context
of this revelation, which is almost enthusiastically ig-

nored, has little if any relation to the traditional academic disciplines, but does speak of one of the most sublime things available to mortals.

The knowledge of which man cannot be ignorant and be saved is knowledge of the truth, that is, Jesus Christ, the Redeemer of the world, and the principles which he has revealed. Not just the principles, but he in addition to the principles does and will make men free. The point is, even with the principles, and without him men could not ultimately be free.

Man finds value in secular truth and no doubt will continue to find value in it; however, without redemptive truth ultimately secular truth will be esteemed as less than sounding brass and a tinkling cymbal by him who has it.

Let us all enthusiastically pursue knowledge, but let us not be deceived by equating knowledge with salvation, nor permit ourselves to be led gently down to hell by equating the gospel of success with the gospel of Jesus Christ. Let us continuously strive for success of the soul. May we desire with all our hearts, in addition to our love of and eager strivings for knowledge, to become in our natures of a celestial character. May we follow the simple yet profound admonition, "seek ye first the kingdom of God, and his righteousness." (Matthew 6:33.)

Index